# IMAGINE THAT...

Reconciling Your Imagination with the Sovereignty of God!

## BRIAN F. FLECK

*Brian F. Fleck*

*Galatians 1:3-5*

Trilogy Christian Publishers
A Wholly Owned Subsidary of Trinity Broadcasting Network
2442 Michelle Drive
Tustin, CA 92780

For information, address Trilogy Christian Publishing
Rights Department, 2442 Michelle Drive, Tustin, Ca 92780.
Trilogy Christian Publishing/ TBN and colophon are trademarks of
Trinity Broadcasting Network.
For information about special discounts for bulk purchases, please
contact Trilogy Christian Publishing.
Manufactured in the United States of America

Cover photo credit: Eddi Aguirre (via Unsplash.com)

10 9 8 7 6 5 4 3 2 1
Library of Congress Cataloging-in-Publication Data is available.
ISBN 978-1-64088-443-4
ISBN 978-1-64088-444-1

To our son, Christopher, who was taken from this life in an instant, leaving our family and friends to experience the true meaning of sorrow. This work, which is a direct result of your death, has comforted your mother and me as we have come to understand how you were a precious seed the Lord has taken and planted. It is our hope that an abundance of fruit will come forth and grow from the tears and grief we've endured along this excruciating journey.

"Verily, verily, I say unto you, Except a grain of wheat fall into the ground and die, it abideth alone; but if it die it bringeth forth much fruit."

John 12:24

# Table of Contents

## SECTION 2

# Introduction

One of my favorite books in the Bible is the Book of Job, because it magnifies the danger of leaning upon our human reasoning when trying to speculate about *how* a Sovereign God deals in the affairs of men. Although Job and his friends stimulate much thought and insight about the Lord's "ways" during their arguments, it's a scary debate to witness as these men mingle their *personal experiences* and *feelings* about God within their imaginations, to draw conclusions about why God allowed such sorrow, suffering, and pain to come upon Job.

If you remember, within just a few hours thieves had invaded Job's three territories and stolen all his cattle and killed his workforce. Then, that which Job feared most happened—all ten of his children were killed in a storm. Shortly thereafter, probably within a day or so, Job finds himself covered in boils from head to toe, stricken with pain and using broken pottery to burst open the swollen sores for relief. Hearing about the horrors Job was enduring, his three closest friends come to visit and spend an entire week—note this—*in silence*, pondering and speculating within their imaginations what the root causes of all his suffering might be.

Their conclusion: Job obviously has done something extremely wicked to deserve all this suffering! Whoa! Talk

1

about judgmental, human reasoning.

Of course all of us find ourselves drifting off into our imaginations on occasion, considering various causes and possible motives, forming our opinions while leaning on our own experiences and feelings to draw conclusions about people and situations. But the question is: Do we realize how attitudes are being formed and planted deep within our hearts during these times of meditation and fantasizing, especially when it comes to making decisions and forming opinions about family, friends, neighbors, and co-workers?

Understanding the pitfalls and dangers that lurk within our imagination, where dress rehearsals come alive whether they be true or not, I'd like to take you on a journey through your mind's eye—your imagination—so you might discover for yourself some good and bad patterns you have established through the years—especially the bad ones, because we all have them.

Now, I do want to warn you. This journey is going to be rough on occasion, because it is going to expose many of your insecurities and attitudes. But, here's the good news: Guess who is going to be sitting right next to you when you hit the potholes, trek the steep hills, and go around those dangerous curves? You got it! The Lord! And before you know it, the journey will be over. And my hope is that you come off this maiden journey ready to get right back on!

# Deceptive Imagery

While walking the alluring boardwalk in Ocean City, Maryland as a teenager in the seventies, my friends and I came upon a huge dome-like structure called the Super 180. Noticing a crowd forming to enter the dome, we decided to buy tickets to see what the attraction was.

When we finally entered the building instructions were given, "Please walk to the railings and find a place behind them. Your Super 180 experience is about to begin."

We then walked over to eight railings that were cemented to the floor. All the railings were about thirty feet long, waist high, and were aligned one in front of the other. It all seemed very odd to me. The place was enormous, but they only allowed forty to fifty people inside for the...whatever we were there for. I had no idea.

Suddenly, the lights went out and a movie was projected onto the wall in front of us. It was a spectacular sight. The movie had us inside an old-fashioned propeller airplane flying about fifty feet above the ground, and we were viewing the horizon of the Grand Canyon. As far as I was concerned, we were literally flying. It was so realistic as I looked out over the wing of the plane admiring the beauty of it all.

Then, without warning, I found out why the railings

were cemented to the floor. The plane we were flying in went out over a cliff, banked to the right, and we were looking straight down into a canyon some three thousand feet deep. Instantly, I grabbed the railing and held on for my life. Everyone else in the building was shocked as well. Although we were standing on a cement floor, we all grabbed the railings. It was so real!

As we continued, we enjoyed the thrills of floating in a hot air balloon and riding a roller coaster and a streetcar in San Francisco. But the one segment that affected me the most was the ride on a trail bike.

As we proceeded through dense woods, we experienced every bump and turn. For me, this was no longer fun. Since I had just finished eating a huge tub of Thrasher's fries before walking into the theatre, my stomach was starting to talk to me. To regain my composure, I had no other choice but to close my eyes. Immediately, my stomach settled down and I was in control.

I guess fifteen seconds elapsed when I reopened my eyes. To my horror, we were still riding the trail bike. I couldn't believe it. In just a matter of seconds I was feeling nauseous again. I then closed my eyes a second time. Shortly thereafter, the movie came to its end and the lights came on.

Are you beginning to understand how controlling and deceptive life's imagery can be? Just think about how influential our imaginations are in our lives, especially when the imagery we view and ponder within our hearts and minds during our alone time becomes a part of who we are and then flows into our relationships.

Therefore, take this to heart:

Everyone possesses the ability to decide what *we will* or *will not* look at and what *we will* and *will not* envision and ponder within our hearts and minds via our imagination. But once we *choose* to yield our imagination to any given imagery, whether in the material world or within our own meditations, we cannot control the effect it will have on us.

Let's read that again:

Everyone possesses the ability to decide what *we will* or *will not* look at and what *we will* and *will not* envision and ponder within our hearts and minds via our imagination. But once we *choose* to yield our imagination to any given imagery, whether in the material world or within our own meditations, we cannot control the effect it will have on us.

This is the reason why the Lord gives us a stern warning about what we meditate upon within our imagination, for He understands the dangers of expanding our emotions toward selfish lusts that will control and war against our body, mind, and soul. And He specifically warned us in Matthew 5:27-28 about getting caught up in lustful fantasies and dreams that we cannot morally fulfill.

"Ye have heard that it was said by them of old time, Thou shalt not commit adultery: But I say unto you, That whosoever *looketh* on a woman *to lust after her* hath committed adultery with her already in his heart."

That's an extremely stern statement. But let's consider what the Lord Jesus said in light of my Super 180 experience.

He declared that "...whosoever *looketh* on a woman *to lust after her* hath committed adultery with her *already* in his heart."

In other words, when a man *purposely* looks at a wom-

5

an with lust and forms imagery within his imagination, he has *already committed the sin of adultery*. How is this possible? Because the emotions stirred by the imagination are genuine, just like the ones I experienced in the Super 180, and they become a part of you.

You see, God has placed this spiritual antenna within our hearts and minds—the *imagination*—which has a direct link to our emotions. So, when our antenna picks up on a thought, a dream, a fantasy, or even a conflict in our relationships that is triggered by what we have seen, heard, or meditated upon, the transmissions instantly arouse our emotions; and too often, our egos, our selfish pride. Then, there is a clash between our emotions and our conscience as we are required to make a distinction between what is right and what is wrong, what is true and what is false.

I challenge you to examine this battlefield within our minds. Please take a moment to read Luke 4:1-13. In a sneaky attempt to gain a stronghold within the Lord's heart and mind, Satan *channels prideful thoughts* into the Lord's imagination, presenting Him with *possibilities* for His future as he did with Adam and Eve in the Garden of Eden. Herein our Lord is teaching us the importance of ignoring the subtle notions that only fuel our pride, insecurities, and doubts while realizing it is God's Word that will lead us to safety in the midst of the battle.

One of the first lessons the Lord taught His disciples in John 8:32 was the importance of seeking truth. Why? Look at the verse:

"And ye shall know the truth, and the *truth shall make you free.*"

Makes us free from what?

Due to the stress and pressures of day-to-day living, many of us misuse and even abuse this God-given antenna, the imagination, which is too often contaminated by our pride, emotions, and selfish motives. We rather enjoy floating off into our little fantasy worlds, planning and strategizing future encounters and events so we might choreograph our actions to our advantage. Once we step into the shadows of our fantasies and dreams, we then convince ourselves that we can somehow turn them into reality by the efforts we envision.

Why do we do this?

Often, we lean upon our imagination to gain a sense of control or even to escape reality's demands. Whether it is within the silence of our cars, a CD, a book, the internet, a movie, or even relaxing in a hot shower, it is during those moments alone that we often find ourselves fantasizing and dreaming about *possibilities* that may lie ahead in our future. But even if our visions of future *possibilities* are rooted in good and godly intentions, the fantasy world we create can still blind us from seeing what God has for us. Too often *our expectations* within our illusive visions can cloud His Will for our lives, which is extremely dangerous and detrimental to our relationships.

This is the reason why our Lord admonished us in Matthew 5:8, "Blessed are the pure in heart: for they shall see God."

You see, God desires that we exercise our imagination with meditation and prayer under the protection of His Guidance so we will focus on truth—*real life* problems and situations that come across our path. In doing this, we will gain the emotional strength and wisdom we need to see beyond ourselves, so we might empathize with others in their struggles. It is our imagination—saturated in prayer and meditation—that will keep our hearts in the realm of reality to promote deeper and more meaningful relationships with our family, friends, and neighbors.

Now, let's go a little deeper so we might understand *how* the thought patterns within our imagination can be detrimental to us and to our relationships. Consider a statement our Lord spoke regarding His returning to the earth. When His disciples asked Him about the signs that would be unveiled before His second coming, our Lord said this in Matthew 24:36 & 37: "But of that day and hour [His second Coming] knoweth no *man*, no, not the angels of heaven, but my Father only. *But as the days of Noah were*, so shall also the coming of the Son of man be."

And what was the culture like in the days of Noah?

Genesis 6:5 tells us, "And GOD saw that the wickedness of man *was* great in the earth, and *that every imagination of the thoughts of his heart was only evil continually.*"

And the Lord added this when speaking with Noah in the same chapter verses 11-13:

> The earth also was corrupt before God, and the earth was filled with violence. And God looked upon the earth, and, behold, it was corrupt; for all flesh had corrupted his way upon the earth. And God said unto Noah, The end of all flesh is come before me; for the earth is filled with violence through them; and, behold, I will destroy them with the earth.

Unfortunately, these characteristics, *"evil imaginations and violence,"* are dominating our culture today and are often displayed with pride and arrogance, even admiration.

Now, as we move forward, there are going to be moments on this journey when you may have to pause to reflect on some harsh conclusions and attitudes you have developed within your own imagination about situations and people that were *later proven totally wrong by reality.* Sadly, what you will discover, as I have, is even though reality has proven you wrong on occasion, any negative opinions and attitudes ignited during those ventures within your imagination have watered seeds of pride, criticism, and resentment that will contaminate future mediations. It can be a very dangerous cycle that, according to the Lord's declaration, can lead to deceptive patterns of fantasy, resentment, hostility, and even violence.

# Persuasive Illusions

Whether a person is entering kindergarten, junior or senior high school, college, or even retirement after working some fifty years, there are always obstacles and challenges sprinkled throughout our lives. They can leave us puzzled, and even irritated at times, especially when the wonder of *who we are* and *why we are here* fuels the mystery of our existence. But what complicates life's challenges and our interactions with people too often, is when we find ourselves drifting into our imagination to rehearse exchanges—simulated events—to ponder questions and situations about our future that may or may not occur or even be true.

Herein is how we can be deceived:

During our meditations about life and circumstances, especially our relationships, we conjure up "possible" encounters or events yet to be determined, which tend to stir up and bring to the surface our deepest emotions and insecurities, along with our prejudices, good or bad, to decide "I'd do this..." or "I'd say that..." or "If I were them, I'd do this..." depending upon what is happening in the vision we've conjured up. Then, within the hodge-podge of possibilities we've considered, we do our best (we really do most of the time) to render conclusions that fit our desired expectations. Sadly, though, this exercise often comes at a greater expense than we realize. For during our "crystal ball moments" to foresee and somehow "control" our future, we not only inflate our expectations and set ourselves up for disappointment, but we tend to justify our selfish attitudes along the journey, especially after pinpointing whatever and whoever may present a threat to "our desired outcome." As a result, negative attitudes, and sad to say, even thoughts of revenge, can fester within our soul toward others and even God as we "strive" to justify our words and deeds within our fantasy world. Ouch!

The world we create within our imagination can be extremely dangerous!

John Locke, a 17th century British philosopher whose writings were a great contributor to the establishment of America's Declaration of Independence and Constitution, said it best:

> "Thus men, extending their enquiries beyond their capacities, and letting their thoughts [*imaginations*] wander into the depths where they can find no sure footing; 'tis no wonder, that they raise questions and multiple disputes, which never coming to any clear resolution, *are proper to only continue and increase their doubts*, and to confirm them at last in a *perfect skepticism*," (John Locke, An Essay Concerning Human Understanding).

Today, "skepticism" has become a dark cloud that overshadows our trust in others, and even in God. It has become an "admirable" characteristic in our culture, which only fuels the imagination toward evil, revenge, and violence within our society.

So, I need to ask the question:

How much of your meditation within your imagination is influenced by skepticism in your effort to find sure footing in the defense of your opinions, interests, and worldview?

The answer is, "Too much," I would venture to say. And why is this so? Keep reading and see if you agree with me.

When people—and that's you and me—are skeptical about an event and the people involved, it tends to inflate our pride, validating *our wisdom* as we convince ourselves that we have a special insight to the possible cause and motives. Thus, skepticism has become a defense mechanism in our minds to pinpoint hidden motives that helps protect us from being taken advantage of in this selfish, greedy world. And while our meditations are easily swayed by our fears, doubts, insecurities, and guilt on occasion, we tend to lean toward negative innuendos, blaming others and making excuses to validate and justify our bad attitudes, and especially our behavior. It is an extremely deceptive cycle we lean on for counsel and comfort that leaves us wandering "into the depths where *we can find no sure footing*," giving testimony to Mr. Locke's warning.

"I know!" Someone is saying, "Just look around you, Fleck! Don't you see what he or she did and what's happening?"

My response, "Well, does the situation, bad behavior, or attitude of others suddenly grant us the unconditional right to do wrong? Are you telling me that our bad behavior and excuses are somehow justified by the bad behavior of others?"

How often do we convince ourselves that they are?

I know. The "hidden" meditations of your heart become a soothing balm to convince you that you are somehow gaining an advantage, and it doesn't matter what anyone else thinks! And with that, the "I don't care" attitude is permeating our culture. Even worse, it is a deceptive cloud that prevents us from dealing with reality and what is true. For whenever I hear someone say, "I don't care!" my conclusion is…they do care, very deeply. But since no one else seems to care, they are left frustrated and hurt thinking, *Then, why should I care?* Understood! I've been there many times myself. But again, why do we allow bad attitudes to influence, or should I say, intimidate, us?

The ultimate danger of such skepticism is the conjuring up of "false assumptions" to validate and justify our negative opinions; and then, we become most comfortable in our pessimism and skeptic view of life. Like Eeyore, we very rarely see through the clouds to experience the brilliance of the sun and its beauty.

Although there are many scriptures that counsel us concerning our imagination and how to control it with the truth of God's Word, I want to first make a transition that will help us gain a greater appreciation for the Lord's counsel when we do visit those scriptures.

Please read Webster's definition of *"imagination"* and consider what we've discussed thus far.

Imagination defined:

*The act or power of forming a mental image of something not present to the senses or never before wholly perceived in reality. 2: creative ability.*

Given this definition, I want to make a very bold statement that will overshadow the remainder of this study. Here it is. Ready…

Nothing; I said, NOTHING, can exist or come into existence APART from someone's imagination!

Whatever can be seen or touched was first envisioned within someone's imagination *BEFORE* it came into being. Whether it be buildings, motor vehicles, cures for diseases, infrastructures in cities, even a harvest on a farm, there was first a vision within someone's imagination that led them to create plans to see the vision come into reality. Why do students suffer the trials and struggles of school and college? To gain the fulfillment of their dream—the goal they've envisioned for their future. Whether it be an occupation, career, or professional sport, each day is motivated and governed by a vision for achievement. Of course, I didn't say every vision we have is exciting. But in order to reach any accomplishment in any given day we must first envision the goal and then make a plan of action to bring about the chosen results.

And please remember this: During this process of forming mental images, we are stirring up and dealing with emotions that can create and feed attitudes that flow into our behavior even though reality has not yet been realized. So, be careful!

Warning: In this next section, it may feel like I have suddenly changed the channel of the television on you, so take a deep breath! However, if what I have just shared with you has stirred your thoughts and the gears are churning and moving into overdrive, feel free to stop and come back later. -For here comes one of those sharp turns I told you about, so hold on!

# Beyond Our Imagination

Setting our imagination and all of what's been stored up in them on the shelf for a few pages, let's apply what we've discussed about the *imagination* to a Holy and Loving, Eternal God who has no beginning or ending.

Oh, and please feel free to use your imagination when thinking about this. In fact, you will need to use it when considering *God is Spirit* and exists everywhere. He is ever present in all places, for He is Almighty God!

Now, if God be God, and I believe He is, what do you think is the # 1 thing God wants us to know and believe about Him? The first verse of the Bible—Genesis 1:1—sets the tone for everything that follows when it clearly states; "In the beginning God created the heaven and the earth."

Before I present my thoughts to you in the next paragraph on this subject and how those thoughts magnify the majesty and holiness of an awesome, loving Creator, please take a few minutes yourself to think about what God must have been imagining out in Eternity Past before He, the Lord God, decided to speak our Universe and the innumerable Galaxies into existence. He, the Creator of all we can see, touch, hear, taste, and smell; the Heavenly Artist, obviously had been thinking, even dreaming for who-knows-how long, about how He could make life exciting, pleasurable, and joyful for the humans He would at last create. And while letting your imagination run wild with that thought, remember my bold statement as you think about God and His dreams for us: Nothing; I said, NOTHING can exist or come into existence APART from someone's imagination!

My conclusion on the matter:

In chapters one and two of the Genesis account of Creation, the Creator of the material world displays everything He had been dreaming about within His imagination for who-knows-how long. The Sovereign, Eternal God of the Universe reveals for all of us to see, what He had been dreaming about and envisioning within His imagination in Eternity Past for us. And this is the very first thing God wants us to know above all else. From the depths of His being in Eternity Past, He envisioned within His imagination and dreamed about how He could best share His Life with others. And then, in His wisdom, He created the heaven and the earth; a perfect environment for humans and the amazing creatures He would create, giving us precious life so we could enjoy and share in His dreams for us.

Again, please keep the following in mind as we seek to understand the Lord and His heartbeat for us when He decided to step from Eternity's Splendor to create matter and time: The Lord God in all His Holiness and Majesty is SPIRIT, a consuming fire, infinitely greater than the Sun He created. Therefore, no one, not even the angels in heaven can approach Him and live. Thus, He created the heaven and the earth to declare His glory (presence) while revealing to us His heart and attributes.

For example: The fact that the sun rises in the east and

sets in the west every day shows He is Faithful to us and that His mercies are new every morning. Yes, the watches and clocks we look at every day are a reminder and reflection of His faithfulness and that He has everything under control.

Of course, there is Psalm 19:1 that proclaims to us, "The heavens declare the glory of God, and the firmament showeth His handiwork."

How? Our solar system and all the galaxies beyond reveal to us that God is eternal. He has no beginning or end and He is present everywhere.

And when I think of how He sprinkled His personality traits into the animal kingdom, I stand in awe. My two favorites are turtles and squirrels. Whenever I watch them in their habitats, I find myself laughing to tears, especially the hyper squirrels. What a contrast! To think that they are but a reflection of God's ingenuity and personality is mind-boggling. I could go on through Genesis to show you His character and attributes within His creative artistry. He is brilliant at what He does! What a Great God! .

Therefore, *if* all of what I have stated is true; that all life He created was and is a mirrored reflection of the Lord God's imagination, then two other things must be true:

First, He is the sustainer of all life. If He did indeed create humans and animals and breathed into all His created beings the very breath for life, then every second of our lives is given and sustained by Him. *He is the source* of each day we have here. Without Him, everything STOPS! Worse...everything dies!

Second, and most importantly, since we have been created by Him—Are you ready for this?—our existence is a reflection and a fulfillment of a dream that was first developed within the Creator's imagination even before the world was created. You and I existed in the heart and mind of God in Eternity Past where He spent—who-knows-how long—dreaming about *the very day* we would be born so He could share the life He has given to us with Him, the Creator and Giver of Life!

Two weeks after my son, Christopher, was instantly killed in a head-on collision caused by a drunk driver, I settled back into work, where I was presented with this profound question while talking about spiritual matters with Christopher's closest friend.

He leaned in toward me and asked, "Where was Christopher before he was born?"

Without hesitation I replied, "In the mind of God."

Then, as the reality of that statement dominated my thinking, I set out with all my heart to gain a deeper understanding of God's Sovereignty and how His Sovereignty truly impacts all of us. The first thing my wife, Carol, and I shared with Christopher's siblings and his wife, Erica, over the weekend Christopher was killed, is this:

"This is bigger than all of us! God has a plan in all this." God has known everything that's going to happen, even before He laid the foundations of the worlds.

Which means, the Lord knew exactly what was going to happen that Saturday, September 23, 2017 at 1:20 p.m., and He had known about it before He created the foundations of the world.

You may be thinking: *And what does all this have to do with my imagination?* Please be patient. We will come full circle in my humble effort to fulfill the purpose of this writing:

Reconciling our Imagination with the Sovereignty of God.

After a year and half of praying, studying, and typing out hundreds of pages of thoughts and notes, here is the main lesson the Lord has been teaching my wife and I after our son's death. During this journey, I have found that all my thoughts and study are constantly being channeled into this one essential truth that is, quite frankly, too often overshadowed by life's heartaches and struggles. This sobering reality is presented to us within Hebrews 4:1-4, especially for the hard times when trials and heartbreak test our soul:

> Let us therefore *fear*, lest, a promise being left *us* of *entering into His rest*, any of you should seem to come short of it. For unto us was the gospel [good news] preached, as well as unto them [*unbelievers*]: but the word preached did not profit them, not being mixed with faith in them that heard it. For we who have believed [*in a Sovereign God*] do enter into rest, as he said, As I have sworn in my wrath, [that they who did not believe] shall never enter into *my rest: although the works were finished from the foundation of the world*. For he spake in a certain place of the seventh *day* on this wise, And
> God *did rest the seventh day from all his works.*

Here is what the Lord is patiently teaching Carol and me, and wants to teach all of us:

We need to learn to *Rest in God's Sovereignty by faith*, just as God Himself rested after He created the heavens and the earth in six days, setting His dreams in motion. And how could the Lord God rest on the seventh day even though life for mankind had just begun? Because *all of time*, which encompasses our material world as we know it—the past, present and even our future—*had, and has, already happened in the mind of God before He created the foundations of heaven and earth.* Even the last chapter of our lives has already been penned by Him though we've not arrived there yet. But for now, time is playing out and revealing our attitudes toward the gift of life He has given us. What are we doing with this gift of life?

You see, being Sovereign [All Powerful], Omniscient [He knows everything] and Omnipresent [He is everywhere], He has the foreknowledge of all the events that are going to occur in each of our lives, and He has pre-determined how He will deal with us based on how we respond to those events. Seem far-fetched?

Remember the movie *Groundhog Day* with Bill Murray? A silly, but great, movie when you consider how the movie magnified God's Sovereignty and how God decides how to deal with people based on His foreknowledge. If you haven't seen it, please rent it and watch it.

Yes, having foreknowledge may seem far out for some of us, but it shouldn't. Even we creatures of dust make plans for our future all the time based on our foreknowledge, just like God does.

For example: I have worked in the manufacturing business all my life. At certain intervals of my career, I was a Production Manager/Scheduler. And if you would allow me to say, a god of sorts within the company. Everyone came to me for the plan and direction. So, based on the demands of our customers, time, and resources, I would work to set in stone a *predetermined* schedule that best helped us achieve our goals. During the planning stage, I would look into the future with my foreknowledge and envision plans within my imagination considering our resources, the talent of our machinists, machine capabilities; and of course, numerous obstacles (outside platers and testing) that might create delays to hinder us from fulfilling the vision I had developed for us. Despite all the planning involved, there were always unforeseen events—a flu epidemic, broken machines, wrong hardware ordered, delayed deliveries from outside vendors, etc.—that would disrupt the fulfillment of our dreams, our goals, our highest expectations. Thus, we had to regroup and make alternative plans so we could fulfill as much of the schedule as possible, despite the obstacles. Later, we would leave our frustration and disappointment behind us, learn from our experience, and then carry lessons learned into the next month, hoping to control whatever we could to reach our future expectations.

Then, there is the planning of our vacations. Think about all the pre-planning you enjoy or disdain within your imagination when considering a vacation. When my wife and I head to the beach once a year, we do our best planning based on our foreknowledge of this venture.

First, we have investigated the best Condos to stay within our budget and we always get a beachfront property. If we're going to the beach, we want to be on the beach. If we're going to the Smoky Mountains, the same holds true! We want a view of the Mountains from our balcony. I don't want to have to drive anywhere!

Second, we plan our vacations to avoid the peak seasons. We want to relax! We want the beach to ourselves. We don't like sharing on vacation. We've gotta deal with life's fast lane all year and this is one time we plan, based on our fore-knowledge, to get away from it all.

Third, based on our foreknowledge, we plan our depar-ture and return at specific times. When headed to the beach we leave at 4:00 a.m. to avoid traffic jams in Washington, DC and Richmond, Virginia. And on our return trip, we usually leave on Friday night so we can avoid the mass exodus on Saturday morning. That way, we get home between 2-4 a.m. in the morning, get 6-8 hours of sleep, and then wake up before noon on Saturday to relax at home before hitting the grind on Monday.

So, think about what we could do in planning our future if we were a Sovereign and Omniscient God—knowing the end from the beginning! What would you do? Rest! Because if we foreknew ALL the obstacles, detours, and cantankerous people who might create delays or disrupt our plans, we could easily make the appropriate adjustments to insure we reached our chosen, predetermined destination.

Therefore, we need to *learn by faith* HOW TO REST in this reality...

Our lives, all your days and mine, and all our tomor-rows, have already happened in the mind of God. Done! And it is the Lord Jesus Christ, who is God come in the flesh, who fulfills ALL the dreams He and His Father imagined in Eterni-ty Past for us, despite the obstacles we and others create in His schedule. He already knows what you and I are going to do. He even knows what we are going to think before we think it! Of course, that doesn't mean each day is going to be a great, rosy-colored day. All of us will experience disappointment, stress, heartache, and sorrow because we live in an unjust and corrupt world that creates and fuels many discouraging events in our lives.

But the question is this:

Will we acknowledge Him in all our ways so we might seek to fulfill the dreams He has planned for us, even during our most challenging moments? Or will we ignore Him, believing we can find our own way, hoping the imaginations of our heart will match up with reality? He's given us His very best, ALL He has. Now, what are we going to do with it?

"Adam!" God shouted when He came to visit him and his wife after they ate the forbidden fruit.

"Adam!"

Oh, that's right. Adam decided he didn't need God's guidance anymore, so he and Eve ate of the tree of knowledge of good and evil which expressed to God that they had everything under control and they can live their lives without Him. They decided they knew what was best and that they had the insight and wisdom to choose for themselves what was right and wrong.

Now, was that what God had dreamed about within His imagination concerning Adam and Eve before He spoke heaven and earth into existence? For them to choose death rather than life?

Certainly not! And yet, He knew before He created the heaven and the earth that they would choose death rather than life. Herein is what confuses us and complicates our view of God most—the fact that a Sovereign Creator would give us a free will, so we might decide for ourselves what is right and what is wrong, knowing full well that we would choose to eat of the forbidden fruit; thus, leading us into heartache, sorrow, grief, and even death.

Why would God hand such power of choice to creatures of dust?

For one reason and one reason only!

So that we humans could decide for ourselves—like Adam and Eve—if we want to believe, trust, and walk with God or run away from Him. Never forget *our choices* reveal what is within our hearts. Our actions are but a reflection of our hearts.

In Revelation 3:20 the Lord gives us a perfect picture of God's heartbeat, how He longs to help and guide us. The Lord Jesus is speaking here…

"Behold, I stand at the door [of your heart], and knock: if any man hear my voice, and *open the door*, I will come in to him, and will sup [fellowship] with him, and he with me."

The Lord God doesn't want a bunch of robots living in the Eternal Home He is preparing for us. He gently knocks on our heart's door seeking entrance, and we make a choice to open it for Him. He will NOT force Himself on any of us. He desires for people to trust and love Him willingly! He longs to have a relationship with people who are excited about Him, and who want to enjoy Him and all that He has for us. Therefore, we choose! Isn't that what makes our marriages exciting? The willingness to be with each other, and the freedom we can share in that "choice" to enjoy each other! Marriage should not be a dictatorship, nor is our relationship with God.

The main problem is we have convinced ourselves we don't need God. Since our culture has provided abundantly for our ease, comfort, and pleasure, our vision of God and having a relationship with Him is often blurred by our prosperity and over-inflated dreams. In our narrow thinking, our material possessions and wealth define our success and who we are. With all we possess, do we really need God for our daily bread? I mean, I can take care of myself. I have enough bread right now for a month! I even have enough to feed the fish and turtles in the pond out back.

Right now, let's really use our imagination within the scriptures to pull all this together. This can easily be done, I think, by considering the choice Adam and Eve made in the Garden of Eden so we might discover what led them to such a bad choice.

Consider this: There was only one temptation in their path. There were no Hollywood distractions, drugs, red light districts, material world to covet, or Wall Street to lure them away from God. There was but one tree—that's it!

Okay, ready! Even though you may have read this passage dozens of times, please read it slowly so you can capture the scene within your imagination.

Genesis 3:1-6 tells us:

Now the serpent was more subtle than any beast of the field which the LORD God had made. And he said unto the woman, Yea, hath God said, Ye shall not eat of every tree of the garden? And the woman said unto the serpent, We may eat of the fruit of the trees of the garden: But of the fruit of the tree which is in the midst of the garden, God hath said, Ye shall not eat of it, neither shall ye touch it, lest ye die. And the serpent said unto the woman, Ye shall not surely die: For God doth know that in the day ye eat thereof, then your eyes shall be opened, and ye shall be as gods, knowing good and evil. And when the woman saw that the tree was good for food, and that it was pleasant to the eyes, and a tree to be desired to make one wise, she took of the fruit thereof, and did eat, and gave also unto her husband with her; and he did eat.

What was the *one rule* God gave Adam and Eve to obey?

"We may eat of the fruit of the trees of the garden: *But* of the fruit of the tree which *is* in the midst of the garden, *God hath said, Ye shall not eat of it [only that one tree], neither shall ye touch it, lest ye die."*

And based on this passage of scripture, what was it that led Adam and Eve to ignore and disobey *God's one rule?* A subtle lie that was planted in the imagination of Adam and Eve by the serpent, Satan.

Satan said, *"Ye shall not surely die,"* despite the fact God said they would!

And notice the subtle innuendo that expanded the lie *to amplify the thoughts of their imagination...*

"For *God doth know* [He has hidden motives] that in the day ye eat thereof, then your eyes shall be opened, and ye shall be as gods, knowing [deciding for yourselves] good and evil."

Satan was so cunning, implying that God was using the tree to keep them from being liberated from His authority so they might have a more exciting life independent of Him.

Now, it needs to be noted here—and this is vital for our

thinking—that this rebellion, this grievous sin, this choice to rebel against God's dream for His children, did *NOT* happen immediately after they were created, on the eighth day or the twentieth, for example. I am convinced, based on the genealogy recorded in Genesis chapter five, that Adam and Eve were around sixty years old when they made this contemptuous choice against God. And, it should also be noted, that *their choice* to sin was not an accident or mistake. It was a *calculated* decision they thought long and hard about after speculating about two things in their human reasoning.

First, they were convinced *they would not die* if they ate the fruit. That's what the Serpent told them, and they pondered that thought for many years. In fact, it's possible they may have seen a few birds or monkeys eat of the fruit of the tree of knowledge of good and evil and nothing happened to them. So, eventually, the death attached to their possible action— eating the fruit—fell off the table of consideration! The threat and thought of dying vanished from their thinking. Death's reality was squeezed out of their hearts and minds by the exciting dreams and possibilities they developed within their imagination.

And second, what does death, dying look like anyway? After living some sixty years, they hadn't seen any evidence of death so maybe the Serpent is telling the truth and God is indeed lying to them.

Consider again how persuasive Satan's "little" seed of doubt and distrust toward God was.

*"For God doth know* that in the day ye eat thereof, *then your eyes shall be opened,* and *ye shall be as gods*, knowing [deciding for yourselves] good and evil."

29

Echoing in their imagination they heard: *So God knows that in the day we eat that fruit, we're gonna be just like Him and we won't need to depend on Him anymore. We can make our own decisions about what is right and wrong. And you know what, now that we think about it, I bet eating the fruit would even be a help to God, so He won't have to worry about us anymore.*

Oh, after they pondered the *false notion* about how God was keeping them from their independence, the excitement of making the choice to eat the fruit just *"seemed so right,"* and their imagination was unleashed. Suddenly, in their mind's eye, endless possibilities would be opened for them, and those possibilities seemed so real, they could see them…*if they would just take and eat!* How deceptive that "little" lie of Satan was!

Which brings us to why we need to believe and trust the Lord if we are going to avoid the pitfalls and dangers of our wandering imagination that leans so heavily upon our fantasies, selfish desires, and human reasoning. And the sooner we realize how our visions of grandeur only distort reality, the better.

Here are two passages of scripture the Lord wants us to memorize and grasp:

Proverbs 3:5 & 6 says, "Trust in the Lord with all thine heart; and lean not unto thine own understanding. In all thy ways acknowledge Him, and He shall direct thy path."

And the Lord gives us the most sobering and stern warning as to why we need to trust Him with all our heart in Jeremiah 17:9 & 10:

The heart *is deceitful* above all things, and *desperately wicked*: who can know it? *I the LORD search the heart, I* try [test] the reins [secret motives] even to give every man according to his ways [choices and behavior], *and* according to the fruit [by-product] of his doings."

Now you need to really hold on, we're going to go over some pretty bumpy territory that you are not accustomed to traveling. Whenever God voices an opinion in His efforts to correct and love on us, we tend to resist Him. But, herein, lies our liberty—true, meaningful freedom. Again, hold on; and please, please don't bail out on me. Stick with me and the final leg of the journey will be smooth sailing. I promise!

Within Jeremiah's warning which proclaims emphatically that our hearts are deceitful and desperately wicked and cannot be trusted, we also see the Lord. And what is the Lord doing?

According to the verse, *He is searching our deceitful and desperately wicked hearts.*

Thus, I have got to ask this question: For what is the Creator of heaven and earth searching within each heart and soul that He dreamed about creating before the foundation of the world?

He is searching our hearts (are you ready for this?) to see *HOW* we will respond to the *TRUTH* He gives us! And then, He makes the next move toward or away from us "according to [our] ways, and according to the fruit of [our] doings." Of course, He already knows how we are going to respond to the truth He gives us for He is Omniscient, knowing the end before the beginning of time. *But He is giving us the choice.* He is letting us decide! And you got it! Don't ever be left wondering if God is pro-choice. Of course, that does NOT mean He endorses every choice we make; and rest assured, He is against many of the evil decisions our nation has been making. But let it also be clear: Within each choice we make, the motives of our heart are revealed.

That's why God allows trials and temptations to visit us on occasion. Although He knows what is in our hearts, *we don't.* And it is during the difficult times in life—the struggles, sorrows, and grief—when our hearts are unveiled to expose to us our frailties and even our sin that He already knows about. And when these events *reveal to us* our sinfulness and our vulnerabilities, the Lord then longs to purify and heal our wounded hearts if we will make the choice to go to Him. The hard times in our lives have been allowed and preordained by God, deemed necessary so we might reset our priorities and focus. It is the harsh realities of life that help us, "Get our heads out of the clouds!" Unfortunately, many people find themselves ignoring, some even raising their fists against, the Lord no matter how hard He knocks on their heart's door!

Now, to gain a better understanding of how the Lord searches and tests our wandering hearts with *truth* so that we might grasp just how deceptive our hearts can be, I want to let the Lord Himself tell a parable He shared with a multitude of people along with His disciples. To clarify what a parable is: It is an earthly story taught by the Lord that conveys to us a spiritual truth. And here is a parable that sent the heads of His disciples spinning:

Jesus taught in Matthew 13:3-9:

> Behold, a sower [farmer] went forth to sow; And
> when he sowed, some seeds fell by the way side,
> and the fowls came and devoured them up: Some
> fell upon stony places, where they had not much
> earth: and forthwith they sprung up, because they
> had no deepness of earth: And when the sun was
> up, they were scorched; and because they had no
> root, they withered away. And some fell among
> thorns; and the thorns sprung up, and choked them:
> But other fell into good ground, and brought forth
> fruit, some an hundredfold, some sixtyfold, some
> thirtyfold. Who hath ears to hear, let him hear.

Knowing everyone was puzzled by the parable; a riddle for most, the Lord Jesus expands upon His teaching for His disciples so they would gain a greater *understanding of how people ponder and respond to truth* when they hear it. As you consider the *four different responses* that people have when they hear the truth—God's Word—see where you are right now in light of the reality that God is gently knocking at your heart's door.

Jesus expounds upon the parable in Matthew 13:18-23 making sure they understand the "seed" is the "word of God" being sprinkled on the hearts of men. Here is His explanation:

> Hear ye therefore the parable of the sower.

> When any one heareth the word [truth] of the kingdom, and understandeth *it* not, then cometh the

wicked *one* [Satan with lies], and catcheth away that which was sown in his heart. This is he which received seed [truth] by *the way side*.

But he that received the seed into *stony places*, the same is he that heareth the word [truth], and anon with joy receiveth it; Yet hath he not root in himself, but dureth for a while: for when tribulation or persecution ariseth because of the word [truth], by and by he is offended.

He also that received seed among *the thorns* is he that heareth the word [truth]; and the care of this world, and the deceitfulness of riches, choke the word, and he becometh unfruitful.

But he that received seed into the *good ground* is he that heareth the word, and understandeth it; which also beareth fruit, and bringeth forth, some an hundredfold, some sixty, some thirty.

So, when you consider this parable under the canopy of Jeremiah 17:10, which tells us, *"I the LORD search the heart, I* try [test] the reins [secret motives] even to give every man according to his ways [choices and behavior], *and* according to the fruit [by-product] of his doings," please do not doubt! The Lord God Himself is constantly; yes, constantly, sprinkling seeds of truth within our hearts to draw us to Himself. And our response to His sowing the seeds of truth reveals to us the condition of our hearts. Again, He already knows our hearts are deceitful and desperately wicked. But what is scary, is many times we don't know what's in our own heart until it is shaken by a trial or temptation that falls in front of our path.

So, where might your heart be settled right now? By the Way Side, on Stoney Places, in Thorns, or are you Good Ground that is soft and fertile for growth?

How important is it that we be considered Good Ground by God, those who accept and believe the truth He gives us? Consider the Lord's response to people who reject the truth He gives them. Although it sounds harsh, He is only trying to wake them up.

In John 8:44 we find Jesus *condemning* the Pharisees for their unbelief and rejection of Him and God's Word. Listen to the condemnation when He rebuked these religious leaders in front of a multitude of people.

> Ye are of *your* father the devil, and the lusts of your father ye will do. He was a murderer from the beginning, *and abode not in the truth, because there is no truth in him.* When he speaketh a lie, he speaketh of his own: for he is a liar, and the father of it.

Ouch! That's a strong indictment against the leaders in the most prestigious religious sect. And His rebuke came in the midst of the people who earlier watched these leaders drop their stones when Jesus said to them, "He that is without sin among you, let him first cast a stone at her" (John 8:7). Now you know *why* the Jews wanted Him killed!

He was clearly revealing to the people these leaders cannot be trusted. Not only are they a bunch of liars who are promoting their own agenda, Jesus is letting the people know that their entire belief system is so corrupt they are behaving just like the father of lies, the devil.

Here is another passage of scripture that gives us a glimpse into God's perspective of a person who comes to realize what the truth is, but then rejects the truth anyway. This is scary.

Romans 1:18-22 gives us tremendous insight...

For the wrath [anger] of God is revealed from heaven against all ungodliness and unrighteousness of men, who *hold the truth in unrighteousness*; [WHY?] Because that which may be known of God is manifest [revealed] in them; for God hath shewed *it* unto them. For *the invisible things of Him from the creation of the world are clearly seen, being understood by the things* [the heaven and the earth] *that are made, even his eternal power and Godhead*; so that they are without excuse: Because that, *when they knew God, they glorified him not as God,* neither were thankful; *but became vain in their imaginations,* and their foolish heart was darkened. Professing themselves to be wise, they became fools.

It is mind-boggling to see how a person can reject the truth *even when they come to know God exists.* How does this happen? According to the verse, their rejection of the truth, even when they come to an acknowledgement of it, occurs within a wandering imagination that has no sure footing.

So, we can conclude from these passages of scripture that a person's skepticism and disbelief toward God, the Creator of the world, is always established and built upon lies. Always! And as we've seen, the propaganda campaign of lies started in the Garden of Eden when Satan made his appeal to Adam and Eve, packaging their "opportunity" in a lie which flooded their wandering imaginations with illusions of grandeur.

Therefore, since Jesus clearly stated that Lucifer was and is the "father of lies," let's consider what is going on in Lucifer's deceitful and wicked heart to see—I hate to say it—what we might learn about ourselves. In Isaiah 14:12-14, the Lord shares with us what Lucifer is thinking about himself despite the fact he knows who God is and literally witnessed God's power when He created the worlds:

> *How art thou fallen* from heaven, O Lucifer, son of the morning! *how* art thou cut down to the ground, which didst weaken the nations! *For thou [Lucifer] hast said in thine heart [imagination], I will ascend* into heaven, *I will exalt* my throne above the stars of God: *I will sit* also upon the mount of the congregation, in the sides of the north: I *will ascend above* the heights of the clouds; *I will be like the most High.*

37

Is Lucifer living in a fantasy world or what? He, a created being, thinks he is going to be like God! He is believing a lie he himself conjured up while floating off in his imagination. So now, we need to answer another question: What exactly was it that aroused Lucifer's imagination to convince himself that he could lead a possible rebellion in Heaven to become God anyway?

In the book of Ezekiel 28:11-18 the Lord reveals to us what inspired Lucifer's deceitful and wicked heart [imagination]. Please read it slowly to grasp God's description of Lucifer...

Moreover the word of the LORD came unto me [Ezekiel], saying, Son of man, take up a lamentation upon the king of Tyrus [*the spiritual king*], and say unto him, Thus saith the Lord GOD; [*describing Lucifer*] Thou sealest up the sum, *full of wisdom, and perfect in beauty. Thou hast been in Eden the garden of God;* every precious stone *was* thy covering, the sardius, topaz, and the diamond, the beryl, the onyx, and the jasper, the sapphire, the emerald, and the carbuncle, and gold: *the workmanship of thy tabrets and of thy pipes was prepared in thee in the day that thou wast created.*

[Lucifer had the ability to play orchestrated music from his very being. We continue...]

*Thou art the anointed cherub* that covereth; and I

have set thee *so*: thou wast upon the holy mountain of God [in Heaven]; thou hast walked up and down in the midst of the stones of fire. Thou *wast perfect in thy ways from the day that thou wast created, till iniquity was found in thee.* By the multitude of thy merchandise *they have filled the midst of thee with violence, and thou hast sinned*: therefore I will cast thee as profane out of the mountain of God: and I will destroy thee, O covering cherub, from the midst of the stones of fire. *Thine heart [imagination] was lifted up because of thy beauty, thou hast corrupted thy wisdom by reason of thy brightness*: I will cast thee to the ground, I will lay thee before kings, that they may behold thee. Thou hast defiled thy sanctuaries by the multitude of thine iniquities, by the iniquity of thy traffick; *therefore will I bring forth a fire from the midst of thee, it shall devour thee*, and I will bring thee to ashes upon the earth in the sight of all them that behold thee.

From this lengthy passage we see that it was Lucifer's pride; his self-sufficient attitude that will lead him to his ultimate doom in the Lake of Fire. When he looked at himself and compared himself with all the other angels, there was—as God Himself declared—none that could compare to him. He was the Anointed Cherub, beautiful and extremely wise. But as he became full of himself, God tells us, *"[His] heart [imagination] was lifted up because of thy beauty, thou hast corrupted thy wisdom by reason of thy brightness."* Lucifer deceived himself with a lie, purposely rejecting the truth—reality—that he was but a created being who was given his beauty and talents by his Creator. He had nothing apart from God! But he convinced himself; better yet, deceived himself, into thinking he was "all that!" and that he didn't need God.

Within this passage of scripture, we are also given a glimpse of what *hell* truly is. God said to Lucifer... "I [will] bring forth *a fire from the midst of thee, it shall devour thee."*

Herein God reveals to us what sparks the flames, the torments of hell. Please, please, please understand this: The suffering and torment people will endure in a literal place called hell was, is, and always will be self-inflicted! God didn't create the Hell within the souls of men. Each person born of woman makes his or her own choices. And DO NOT be mistaken, for God has indeed created a literal place called Hell where He ushers and quarantines all those who have chosen to live in that state! For everyone who decides they do not need or want God and have made a choice to reject God's Son, the Lord Jesus Christ, who died for their sins that they might have a New and Resurrected Life in Him, God is going to grant to them their wish—their greatest desire!

And what is a sinner's greatest desire toward God and His laws? They echo the very heartbeat of Adam...

"God, just leave me alone! I don't need You! I like who I am! I'm a good person and I don't need your rules or approval! Again, just leave me alone! I will run my own life"

And that is exactly what God will do for anyone who rejects the truth about His Son, the Lord Jesus Christ.

Sadly, when the Lord leaves a person alone, placing them in an isolated place called Hell that will one day be thrown into a Lake of Fire, he or she will have to face the realities of the actions *they have personally chosen.* The choices, deceptive dreams, and vain expectations they created within the imagination of their heart will torment them forever. That's where hell begins and is fueled. So, when a person decides they will be their own god, rejecting God's forgiveness that comes from the Lord Jesus Christ's death on the Cross, then that's what God allows them to do!

Although I could share dozens of scriptures with you showing what the Lord said about Hell and the importance of trusting and believing in Him to avoid it, let's look at a place that was for many prisoners, hell on earth. I think this place gives us a clear picture of what Hell is going to be like. And I tend to believe the Lord purposely gave us a picture of Hell with Alcatraz, once a prison set on a tiny island surrounded by shark-infested waters.

Based on what we have studied thus far, what do you think the most torturous affliction a prisoner was haunted by and endured while being confined to Alcatraz? Think about it a minute before moving on. Imagine for a moment that you are confined for the rest of your life to this prison looking out beyond the island over shark-infested waters. What are you seeing and thinking about?

I believe what tormented the prisoners most was being able to view the spectacular beauty of San Francisco's skyline across the bay *and knowing* that he would never, ever, ever, ever be able to walk in the freedom of going there to eat the food and drink or enjoy the festive atmosphere he had once shared with other people. Not one more time! Ever!

All a prisoner had to focus on in his isolation were the memories he had stored up throughout his lifetime. And sad to say, many thoughts of regret and guilt would forever torment and haunt him, along with any fantasies of one day possibly being set free from the prison [hell] he had created for himself inside the solitary confinement where he had been sent.

The prison of isolation, a literal place called Hell, that God has established for unbelievers is not good. It is a place of self-inflicted torment—forever! Jesus warned us on many occasions that there will be much wailing and gnashing of teeth. And, as you have imagined, what will make this place so torturous and agonizing is what a person carries with them into Hell. Once there, they will have nothing to entertain them and nowhere they can go to escape. They will be left to lie in the bed they have made for themselves while they were here on earth.

Now, it is important we take a few steps back to examine how the deep-seated *pride* we harbor within our hearts can contaminate our thinking, especially when letting our imagination wander.

And please carry this verse that Solomon gave us in Proverbs 14:12 with you…

"There is a way which seemeth right unto a man, but the end thereof *are* the ways of death."

# Shattered Expectations

When our children were younger, we always enjoyed our Friday nights making popcorn and watching a movie together. On one occasion my oldest son Christopher, who was four years old at the time, wanted to help me make the popcorn. Back in the day, we made it the old-fashioned way in a pot on the stove. We did not own a microwave. And since Christopher always enjoyed helping me, I placed a chair in front of the stove where he was able to stand and oversee the popping process.

The first step in this process required me to melt down butter-flavored Crisco in a huge pot. Once the Crisco was fully melted and the pot well-heated, I then placed a good amount of corn into the pot, making certain I didn't pour in too much.

In a few minutes the corn started popping rather slowly. But suddenly, within one swift moment, the corn began popping so rapidly the sound resembled the firing of a machine gun. This sound was the attraction for Christopher, of course. And before we knew it, the popcorn finished popping and the lid was lifted off the pot some two inches above its rim. Orville was right. He does make the best popping corn.

Now that Christopher and I had enjoyed our shared experience, I turned to get a bowl from one of the cabinets located to the left of the stove above the sink. As I turned to reach for the bowl, I glanced back at Christopher just in time to see him reach forward to touch the heated pot.

"Christopher, don't touch that!" I said firmly. "That's extremely hot and it will burn you."

Since Christopher and I always enjoyed kidding one another, he just smiled at me and reached out in jest to prompt another response from me.

"Christopher, I mean it Bud. Don't play around," I insisted. "It's hot and it will burn you."

I then proceeded to explain to him how dangerous it was to touch a pot on the stove. I explained to him how the red coils on the stove transferred the heat to the pot and the heat then caused the corn to heat up and explode. But after experiencing the excitement of the corn popping, he was under an illusion that there was more to what I was telling him. So, he continued smiling and jokingly reached out again to touch the pot.

I explained to him very carefully a third time how dangerous it can be to touch anything that is on the top of a stove. I even dramatized what would happen.

I said, "If you touch it, this is what will happen."

I reached out to touch it and then quickly pulled my hand back pretending it had burned me. Then I acted like I was crying and told him, "That's what will happen."

To my amazement, he seemed to doubt everything I was telling him. He was determined to find out for himself.

So, I said to him, "Christopher, you now have a decision to make. You can either trust what I'm telling you, or you can ignore what I'm saying and learn the hard way. What do you want to do? Are you going to trust me and believe what I'm telling you? Or are you going to ignore me and touch the pot?"

With a big, confident smile, he pointed at the pot.

"You really want to touch it?" I asked in disbelief.

He continued smiling and shook his head, "Yes."

Given that Christopher obviously refused to trust what I was telling him, I had to prove to him that I was NOT misleading him. I needed to remove all doubt.

"Christopher," I said, getting his undivided attention. "If you really want to touch that pot, I'm going to let you. But it is going to bite you and hurt you. Do you understand that?"

He smiled and shook his head in the affirmative thinking he had everything under control. I guess he needed to find out HOW hot is hot???

I told him. "Go ahead, then. Touch it."

Yes, my little Adam touched the forbidden pot and burned his fingers. The eyes of his understanding were then opened, as he suddenly realized that my words were indeed true. Of course, I felt sorry for the little guy when he let out a blood-curdling scream, confirming all my warnings.

I immediately picked him up from the chair, took him to the sink, and placed his fingers under cold water. After a few minutes of comforting him, the tears began to dry. Then, I sat down with him at the kitchen table, placing him close to my side.

"I told you if you touched the pot it was going to burn you, didn't I?" I gently reminded him.

With his lower lip draped over his upper lip he shook his head up and down, agreeing with me, but I noticed something strange in his eyes. He was *noticeably angry with me*. His eyebrows were conveying to me that it was somehow my fault he had burned his fingers. He was blaming me for his pain.

"Why are you angry with me?" I asked in wonder. "I tried three times to keep you from touching it."

He humbly shrugged his shoulders, letting me know he really didn't understand why. But he was, indeed, angry with me.

At this point, I was so shocked by his angry demeanor that I honestly didn't know how I was going to convey to him the importance of listening and obeying me when I gave him instructions or suggestions. In light of the fact I had failed to convince him to "touch not the pot," how was I ever going to make my point? So, I started praying within my heart, *Lord, please give me wisdom to use this situation to help Christopher understand that I love him and that he needs to trust me whenever I tell him something.*

At this point I looked at Christopher and placed the responsibility back on him. "Do you know why you ignored me and touched that pot?"

Christopher looked at me in wonder, his lip still quivering as he shook his head left to right.

I then told him bluntly, "The reason you touched that pot, and the reason you are now angry with me is because you have sin deep within your heart."

Of course, being but four years old he looked at me like I had ten heads. I thought to myself, "Great! Now how am I going to explain to a four-year-old what sin is?"

Although I honestly didn't know what else to do at this very moment, one thing was sure. I had Christopher's undivided attention, so I continued praying within my heart, asking God for wisdom to work it all out. (Please note: This event would prove to be one of those lasting, defining, positive moments in our relationship for years to come.)

"Christopher, do you know what sin is?" I asked, still wondering where this exchange would lead.

He shook his head, "No."

"Sin is a problem you have in your heart," I said. And then it hit me like a ton of bricks as the Lord honored my prayer of desperation.

"Sin is a problem you have deep within your heart that makes you think you're smarter than me. And you do think you're smarter than me. Don't you, Christopher?"

With his lower lip still draped over his upper lip, he didn't hesitate to shake his head, "Yes." He was totally convinced that he was smarter than his thirty-two-year old father.

Ignoring the temptation to laugh as I was delighting in the Lord's direction, I asked him calmly "But are you really smarter than me?"

He said, "No."

"And yet, you think you're smarter than me, don't you?" I questioned him, lifting my brow.

Again, he shook his head, "Yes."

At this point, I found myself giving the following counsel to my son, and I soon realized God was reminding me about trusting Him in my own life.

"Christopher," I said solemnly as he was looking me square in the eyes, "That's how dangerous sin is. You know you're not smarter than me, and yet you think you are. And do you know what is even worse? Sin will make you think you're smarter than God. And whenever you think you're smarter than God, sin will burn you and hurt you every time!"

During this conversation, I took the opportunity to stress the importance of trusting what I say. Christopher didn't have to endure this experience to understand what I was telling him was *true*. Had he just listened and trusted what I said, "The pot is hot and it will burn you. Don't touch it," he would have been spared the pain, as well as the misguided assumption that blamed me for his problem. And yet, it was through the pain and humiliation sparked by his foolish choice that Christopher came to understand my heartbeat and love for him more clearly. It's somewhat of a mystery we can only experience, but not fully understand…how *love* exposes and covers a multitude of sins to create intimacy. It's great!

Unfortunately, we are too often no different than my four-year-old son when we make unwise choices and get burned by life. When reality does NOT line up with our expectations, hopes, and dreams, our first reaction is often bewilderment and shock which then drives our emotions toward frustration, disappointment, discouragement, and even anger toward God at times.

Why would we get angry with God, the One who supposedly loves us supremely?

Because in the spiritual realm there is always a clash of wills being unveiled —God's and ours! Although many of us work extremely hard to live right to avoid conflict and problems, making honest and good decisions that will benefit us, our family, and friends, we feel great disappointment when our good intentions fall short of our expectations. Even though reality tells us that life—more often than not—is not going to line up with the hopes and dreams we've envisioned within our imagination, we somehow feel slighted and take the detours set before us personally. So, be careful! Too often, we set ourselves up for great disappointment with our planned expectations. Life is always going to throw us curve balls when we least expect it. And when a detour suddenly appears in our path, we must remember this: Most likely it was God Himself who allowed it to be there in order to keep us from a greater danger on the road ahead of us.

So, when financial ventures fall through, unexpected delays occur, and even when family and friends disappoint you, just pray and get God in on it. And then, REST in the reality that He knew about your disappointment before He even created the heavens and the earth. I know. Easier said than done. But He is trying to get our heads out of the clouds of illusion we lean on while revealing to us His heart, that has also experienced shattered dreams, disappointment, and more suffering than we can comprehend.

Then, of course, there are those crushing moments in our lives that are self-inflicted.

As a father, co-worker, and friend, I often remind folks while reminding myself…

"Life is hard enough no matter how hard we try to live right. So why would anyone purposely make bad decisions and make life even harder?"

I can't tell you how many times I've told fellow employees who are having financial problems, "Just come to work when you are supposed to, and you'll be amazed at how 90% of your problems will go away."

And then there are those snap decisions we make that convince us we can enhance our lives with a new "this" or new "that" because "we deserve it!" only to realize later that our decision was made at a greater cost than *we imagined.* Suddenly, we find ourselves carrying an array of attitudes and disappointments that surfaced as a result of our compulsive decisions.

Now that we have a better understanding of *how* our pride influences our decisions, attitudes, and perspectives toward people and situations when flowing through our imaginary previews of events yet to come, I trust you have, as I often do, realized just *how gullible our own intellect can be.* When our imagination is set free to explore all the angles and possibilities; oddly, we can talk ourselves into whatever we deem "right in our own eyes."

Throughout my life I have been given great advice, particularly in my youth. Advice that, had I listened, would have benefited me greatly at that phase of my life, especially financial advice. Of course we all admire and like honesty, even when our family and friends are blunt with us at times, expressing their opinions that may contradict ours. At least they're being honest, even if we don't agree. And yet sometimes, even when we know they're right, we'll ignore them just to try to prove them wrong! Oh, how many times have we all been bitten on the proverbial during those ventures? And as we have seen, this contradiction is usually most intense within parent-child discourses.

But what about when a Loving God is honest and truthful with us, warning us in Proverbs 8:36, "But he that sinneth [rebels] against Me wrongeth his own soul."

What exactly is tucked in that verse? God hates our sin because it hurts us, not Him. God is NOT a control freak! The Lord knows and understands the hell [rebellion] that lies deep within our souls, and *He wants us to understand it* and avoid it!

This is why He tells us in Proverbs 4:23:

"Keep [guard] thy heart with all diligence; for out of it *are* the issues of life."

Certainly, we have just walked through some deep spiritual waters, dealing with eternal issues that you may or may not be comfortable with. Now, we're going to wade through shallower waters we are familiar with so we can—based on the road we've just traveled—examine some of life's choices that can deceive us into thinking we don't need God and we have life under control without Him. Just as Lucifer's position, being the anointed cherub possessing God-given talents *deceived himself* into thinking he could live independently of God, it is vital that we consider *how* our choices often inflate our pride, emotionally and spiritually affecting our hearts  which the Lord clearly tells us we need to *guard with all diligence.*

# Emptying the Recycle Bin

In order to gain a greater appreciation of how our hearts and minds are affected by the choices we make, consider how computers receive and process data. With the evolution of the computer age upon us, it is not difficult for us to accept the fact that our mind—the brain—is, and always will be, the most sophisticated computer and video recorder known to man. As such, we have the means to record life's activities with our video recorder which are then stored within the memory files of our computer. Once our collection of memories has been placed on our memory files, we then have the liberty to enjoy them over and over again, even sharing them with family and friends.

Whether it is an exciting last play of a major sporting event such as the Super Bowl or the Stanley Cup Playoffs, childhood memories, an inspiring movie, or a special occasion that deeply touched us, we have within our computer [the brain] the capability to store "video" footage of our entire lives; and with that, the capacity to recall any experience so we can relive it at will.

There is, however, an unpleasant reality that looms within this splendid feature of our brain with which we must learn to cope. We do not have the ability to delete our errors in judgment or distasteful events of our past which end up being channeled into the recycle bin of our mind's hard drives. Therefore, this limitation—*our inability to erase the negative footage from our recycle bins*—can stimulate destructive viruses such as fear, doubt, and guilt that produce anger, envy, anxiety, stress, pessimism, paranoia, remorse, resentment; even a hatred for others that can overwhelm and infect our hard-drives. This inability makes life extremely difficult at times. Is this fair? No! But it is a reality we cannot change. We do not have a "delete" option readily available within our current programming. There are no existing options from which we can choose to empty the recycle bin so we might free up the valuable space we have wasted.

While this constraint creates limitations within our lives, it is no surprise we find ourselves spending much of our time wrestling with various attitudes (viruses) within our system in an effort to somehow quarantine them. But it is impossible. Whether we like to admit it or not, these viruses, if not dealt with properly, will continue to influence our hearts and minds; yes, even write the scripts we envision within our imaginations. These scripts impact our daily lives and will ultimately influence crucial decisions regarding our future. Unfortunately, this wrestling match only leads us toward frustration, confusion, and resentment. For whenever we fall short or react in a manner that is deemed inappropriate by our conscience; which by the way is God's anti-virus system within our computer, we are then forced to decide how we are going to cope with the negative viruses associated with our flawed ventures. More importantly, how are we going to keep those viruses from governing our hearts and lives and flowing into our relationships?

Herein lies the reason modern day psychiatry and psychology have flourished in our culture. Dr. Phil and others in their respective fields have discovered the bitter realities of this condition, and they know that people are struggling with their relationships because of events that have occurred in their past. This is the reason why professional counselors spend much of their time probing into the past of their clients. They want to "push" this button or that button to uncover what has been hidden in the recycle bin of their client's computer.

But the dilemma these doctors struggle with the most is this:

Once they have finally double-clicked the recycle bin icon and successfully opened it up, their discoveries then point them to a group of other program files their clients have previously installed along life's journey. During the next few sessions, the clients, to their utter amazement, will come to realize it is their attempts at trying to control the viruses that have only compounded their anxiety and depression. The doctor, then, will have to sort through the inner conflicts of their clients to help them understand *how* their attempts at using a variety of deceptive software packages, which have been endorsed by our culture, have only multiplied their heartaches, anxiety; and in some cases, hostility and resentment.

Here are a few of those packages our culture deems viable for our success, setting them before us for our consideration.

## Religious Devotion

This software package is a rather popular one that many people have chosen to install on their hard-drives. In doing so, they believe this package will help them avoid the false hopes and distorted fantasies that permeate our environment today. Many of us have chosen *religious devotion,* believing it will bring clarity and definition to our lives. The Ten Commandments, as outlined in Exodus chapter twenty, is a timeless package we believe we can utilize to help us make "right" decisions for life.

But despite our best intentions, we find ourselves disappointed and heartbroken as we often fall short of its demands upon our lives. As a result, this software package has within it the potential of producing enormous amounts of guilt that will only overload our hard drives and interfere with our relationships. I realize this may cause some theologians to balk, but please keep reading. I'll clarify my point soon.

## Wealth's Magical Wand

*Materialism & Greed* has become a software package that provide an assortment of possibilities when installed. Although it has been around for thousands of years, this package was redesigned and magnified during the 1980s. As America began prospering under the Reagan Administration, the images of greed were planted deep within our hard drives, creating the illusion that our happiness and success in life was dependent upon our purchasing power. Our marriages and children became a secondary consideration as our houses, cars, boats, clothing, jewelry, condos, and season tickets to sporting events quickly became status symbols within our neighborhoods and friendships.

So, to polish our images, we began *working* extremely hard to get the latest updates this package offered. Our focus on our financial portfolios convinced us that the end game (financial freedom) can be justified by any means. As long as we can update this package on a regular basis to sustain the "freedom" to buy and sell, the benefits of this software promised to soothe any ill-gotten gains and broken relationships it created.

Of course, the main problem with utilizing this package to magnify and maintain our self-image is the game never ends. We become so obsessed by the journey and the ambitious quests that we are never satisfied with the prize we sought so hard to gain. Despite all the chosen destinations we may reach, we always come to the end of one road finding another we believe must be taken. Something new comes on the market, and we just gotta have it!

## The Music Industry

The *music industry* has also created a variety of packages to help lead us around the demands and frustrations of life. The strumming of our emotional strings not only promises to soothe our troubled spirits, it also gives us an avenue to reach out to others and share our life philosophies and feelings. Within each song we enjoy there is a truth we can relate to and apply to our everyday life. It becomes a comfort to know there are others in this world who have the same feelings and hold the same beliefs as we do.

But again, the seductive sounds that arouse visions within our hard-drives, like others, can only leave us with feelings of emptiness and heartache as we realize the "real" world doesn't quite line up with all the songs we'd like to sing. Sure, we can find some degree of satisfaction and peace as we slide each song into the channels of our minds. But once the song stops and we walk back into the real world with all its demands, we are often left feeling quite insignificant. Sure, we dream about writing our own songs, but no one really wants to listen to them. Our songs just don't seem to measure up. So we continually play the songs other people write, trying to align our thinking up with theirs, believing that they are the embodiment of success.

## Entertainment

This software package is one of the most dangerous that has evolved over the last fifty years. With the invention of video games, our children run to this illusive world each and every day. Why? It is an avenue of escape that stimulates a sensation of being in control. Floating off into their land of wonder, they feel a sense of achievement and victory. Of course, they are programming themselves for disaster, for I am convinced that many of our learning disorders are tied to these action videos. These games have their minds running in overdrive. Therefore, life outside of their games is boring and unchallenging. And since they do not have the maturity or ability to downshift from their accelerated state, they lose the ability to focus on the facts and figures they need to learn to gain knowledge for life's challenges.

## Drugs

*Drugs* have now become a viable resource that are being taken by users to help them sort through the numerous viruses that have infiltrated their hard drives. Unfortunately, many users take the drugs to escape reality rather than deal with it. So, with each and every puff, pill, prick, and sniff, they believe they are creating a pathway that will take them away from the stress and struggles of life.

The pharmaceutical industry has even legitimized our "mental illnesses" to help us adapt to this lifestyle. They have convinced us that our woes can be soothed by this medication or that one. Sadly though, reality has a way of creeping up on us. Our dependency on the empty promises that lie within the bottle will force us to sacrifice everything we have in our pursuit of a state of contentment.

## Alcohol...Adult Beverages

Although many may not readily agree with me, drinking alcohol—like having sex—is perceived to be a passage to adulthood by our teenagers. It has become a source of enlightenment that leads them across the bridge of discovery toward sensual pleasure. Well, that's what my television is telling me. Drinking is a blast. It is an activity that will lead us to sensual gratification and fun.

Of course, the Lord has made it clear. There is pleasure in sin...for a season. But the sad reality is drinking alcohol has become a primary source some adults use in dealing with their problems, and its usage is obviously taking its toll on our families, and on all of society. For once individuals settle into a habit of consuming two, three, or even more drinks, this ritual then gives them a false sense of security. Suddenly, they have the boldness to accept, and even justify, their methods in resolving their inner conflicts and haunting concerns. In their intoxicated (relaxed) state, they believe they can reconcile their emotional stress with their intellectual reasoning. But Proverbs 20:1 warns us, "Wine is a mocker, strong drink is raging: and whosoever is deceived thereby is not wise."

How deceptive is alcohol? Extremely! Consider the progression.

When a person is sober, he or she is at their fullest capacity to think properly, having their intellect reign over their emotions and body. I realize that thought alone can be scary for some of us. But when a person begins drinking alcohol, the alcohol enters the bloodstream and is then pumped to the brain by the heart. During this process, the alcohol stimulates and even energizes the emotional portion of the brain, while putting the intellect to sleep. So, once a person consumes a drink or two, three, or more, the emotions take control and lay the intellect into a dormant state, putting one's conscience to sleep as well.

The net result: With the spirit of a child our little social drinker will begin saying and doing things he or she would not normally approve of. Suddenly, they feel liberated from their inhibitions. In their mind, they are now invincible. There is nothing they can't do, or at least be willing to try. All obligations and responsibilities become secondary to whatever inflates their ego, for they have found inspiration to venture into an allusive world of empty promises to somehow make their fantasies come true.

The next morning arrives, however, and a reversal takes place. Their emotions are shocked into reality by guilt, since their intellect and conscience are wide awake. Now they are forced to deal with the consequences of their inappropriate actions and any misspoken words they may have uttered. And yet, their ego will not allow them to be beaten down. Knowing what they have discovered about themselves via the alcohol, they will continue to engage in the same behavior, believing all the while they will be able to control the circumstances the next time with the knowledge they have gained *from the guilt they experienced.* Crazy!

# Intoxicating Brews

In Habakkuk 2:5, we have a very interesting verse God has given to help us understand the dangers of becoming intoxicated and where it will lead. This powerful verse has helped me greatly in understanding just how dangerous life can be when we choose to use deceptive and faulty software packages in our effort to resolve our inner conflicts.

The Lord tells us, "Yea, also, because he transgresseth by wine, he is a proud man, neither keepeth at home, who enlargeth his desire as hell, and is as death, and cannot be satisfied..."

Although this passage is emphasizing the dangers surrounding a person's dependency upon wine to enhance his life, the truth is the same could be said regarding every course of sin. Why is this true? Because the key word in this verse is not "wine," but the word "transgresseth." For the person who transgresseth (ignores God's directives) in any area of his or her life instantly becomes susceptible to becoming intoxicated by the emotional stimuli that promotes the *"feel good"* philosophy our culture deems so precious. Then, once an individual is captivated; better still, "intoxicated," and consumed by an idea or impulse that feeds the insatiable ego with fortune, fame, or pleasure, they will find themselves swirling around in the cycle of death, seeking independence to somehow gain greater "opportunities" even at the expense of their own family. Why? Because deep down in their hearts they feel *dead* and they are desperately seeking avenues to obtain a level of adrenaline to make them feel they are alive.

Please take note: There is nothing wrong with playing video games, listening to music, having money, or having goals toward getting a good job and having a better lifestyle. I hope you do have such goals. Goals are important. But do not sacrifice yourself and your relationships in the process. It really doesn't matter what the intoxicant is. Whether it is wine, that promotion, fortune, material possessions, sexual gratification, or popularity, the end result is the same *if these intoxicants consume us* toward satisfying our egos. Soon after we have enjoyed our pleasure in them for a season and come up feeling empty, we will find ourselves back on the same old road groping about searching for the inner peace, joy, and contentment we thought we might secure and maintain. But the reality is: As long as we believe the "things" of the world can define "who we are" via an emotional high, this is the Lord's warning, please listen and heed it:

Our hearts will only be enlarged *as hell* and we will never *be satisfied.*

Please pardon my poetry, but here's a poem I'd like to share with you. I wrote it shortly after I entered college in 1982. I was three years old in the Lord.

## Double-Mindedness

Life is rather simple, yet so complex.
Decisions we make that produce much regret
We know the right answers as a child in a class
Then why do we fail; by success we walk pass.

Our emotions they vary and yet not a few
The person who trusts them frustration's his due
Possessions, they blind us and bind us the same
By the pleasure they brought us, the first time they came.

We get all that we want. Then, why are we blue?
Our God, He's not in them. His joy we once knew.
For all that one gets there's no peace or joy found,
Lest God is the Giver, His grace can't abound.

Yes, He alone holds our joy, our peace, and our hopes.
To trust in earth's riches, we are bonafided dopes.
We buy and we sell and sell and we buy.
Never knowing God's best, we'll just lay down and cry

Eternity's coming and one thing's for sure.
We'll stand before Jesus, the Savior, the Door.
Then, eternity will echo the words we have said
"I sure wish I had," or "I'm sure glad I did."

And this connects to what the Apostle warned us about
in I John 2:15-16:
*Love not* the world, neither the *things* that are in the

world. If any man love [is intoxicated/obsessed with] the world, the love of the Father is not in him [they lose their capacity to love]. For ALL that is in the world, the *lust of the flesh*, the *lust of the eyes*, and *the pride of life is not* of the Father, but is of the world.

This is the reason we need to lean upon God and trust Him to guide us through our dreams and visions for our lives. For if we fail to trust Him and rush headlong into a world of vain promises, forming and chasing illusive dreams within our imagination to find peace and happiness in their subtle notions that are not rooted in *truth*, all we will find is a superficial hope that will have our heads spinning in the cycle of death.

And please realize this one truth as we move forward:

All, not one or two, or even some, I said ALL our fantasies, hopes, and dreams—our perspective of life—have already been programmed and fixed in our brains [computers] during the crucial years of adolescence. And what manipulates and distorts our reality most is our deep-seated fears, doubts; and quite often, guilt, that has also become a part of us through our experiences and reasoning in our youth. Accept this reality or not: the thought patterns and habits established within our memory files during our teenage years have the potential to enslave us and become the master of our destiny.

As stated, our brain possesses a finely-tuned hard drive that God has given to every human being. It is, therefore, this brilliantly designed mechanism that gives us the capacity to reason and make decisions for living. And within this marvelous computer we call the brain, both men and women have a free will. Every one of us have choices we must make. In any given situation, we choose what is right to do, or we can choose what is wrong. It is entirely up to us.

A sobering reminder: The Lord God already knew what decisions you and I were going to make even before we were born! And even when we make a wrong choice to sin against His will for our lives, He is going to do ALL He can do to make our terrible decision work on our behalf. But we need to be willing to listen to His "still small voice." (See 1 Kings 19:11-12.) It will guide us around and through our anxiety, disappointments, and even our resentment. Are you listening?

So as we move toward the finish line, understanding that our minds are indeed the greatest computers ever created, what do you think is going to equip a person so that he or she will have the capability to make "right" choices in life? That's correct. You're getting it! It is the software package he or she chooses to download into the hard drive of their brain.

# An Excellent Choice

As we have already analyzed some of the world's software packages to draw obvious conclusions, we need to revisit the *package of religion,* which I hinted earlier, has a few dangers within its files. And, I believe, the best teacher on this subject is the apostle Paul, alias Saul, who was so dedicated to his religion he justified killing anyone who threatened his belief system.

Prior to his salvation experience on the road to Damascus, recorded in the Book of Acts chapter nine, Saul was a man who whole-heartedly bought into the package of *religion* hoping he might secure his identity and find definition for his life. He cherished his religion and protected it to the fullest. But listen to what he said about himself in Philippians 3:4-6, once he realized how vain and shallow his life had become despite his noble efforts to exalt "religious values" in his life. This is amazing. Please read it carefully. And by the way, Paul wrote this from a jail cell where he was incarcerated for his faith in Jesus Christ. Now, speaking about his old religious beliefs, he wrote:

Though I might also have confidence [to glory or brag] in the flesh. If any other man thinketh that he hath whereof he might trust in the flesh [pertaining to Judaism], I more: Circumcised the eighth day, of the stock of Israel, of the tribe of Benjamin, an Hebrew of the Hebrews; as touching the law [of God], a Pharisee; Concerning zeal, persecuting the church [those who believed in Christ]; touching righteousness which is in the law, blameless.

Paul was reminding the Philippian believers that if they ever wanted to challenge an individual's devotion toward his "religious" pursuits and causes, there wasn't another person in his day who could have touched the hem of his garment. Not only was he born of the priestly stock of Israel, he was a Pharisee among the pharisees. He was the Big Dog in the most honored and sacred denomination. In fact, Paul had learned everything he knew about God and religion at the feet of Gamaliel, who was the Professor of professors regarding God's Law, a man held in great esteem (Acts 5:34). Paul, if you will allow me to say so, would have been just a few steps away from becoming the Pope. That's how dedicated he was to his religion.

But despite all his heritage, his education, and his accomplishments as a religious leader within his community, Paul went on to say in Philippians 3:7 & 8:

But what things [achievements] were gain [precious] to me, those I counted loss for Christ. Yea, doubtless, and I count all things but loss for the excellency of the knowledge [truth] of Christ Jesus my Lord: for whom I suffered the loss of all things,

and do count them *but dung* [manure], that I may
win [attain] Christ.

Once Paul beheld the powerful, risen Savior, the Lord
Jesus Christ, he considered his upbringing, his education, and
all his outstanding accomplishments *"but dung."* How could
he go from one extreme to another? Please lean in and listen!

He came to realize he could not resolve the mystery of
his identity crisis, *Who am I? Why am I here?* with any of the
assorted software packages the world had to offer him, not
even religion. He finally came to understand that they were
useless and worthy of the dung hill when compared to the
*truth* God had for him in Jesus Christ, the Lord.

So once Paul's heart was settled and spiritually sober in
his new-found faith in the Lord Jesus Christ, the Lord not only
opened Paul's spiritual eyes to the Old Testament scriptures
that had prophesied about Christ's coming to die and be resurrected for our sins; but the Lord also had Paul write a number
of books to give us greater insights for living as well. And
one of the most powerful books Paul wrote was the book of
Romans. In this book, Paul gives us detailed instructions as to
*how* we can delete and avoid the destructive viruses of sin that
contaminate and deceive our hearts, and then install the Lord's
software package into our hard drive—our heart and mind—
so we might gain a greater capacity to love, while finding the
peace and joy we long to experience along life's journey.

As we move forward, please understand that this segment of our journey is pivotal. So please, take your time and
reread some paragraphs if needed, to get the full impact of
what the scriptures are telling us.

71

Here, in Romans 12:1-2, Paul presents us with the guidance we need:

> I beseech you, therefore, brethren, by the mercies of God, that ye present your bodies a living sacrifice, holy, acceptable unto God, which is your reasonable service. And *be not conformed to this world: but be ye transformed by the renewing of your mind,* that ye may prove [experience] what is that good, and acceptable, and perfect will of God.

Notice how Paul beseeches [begs] us, according to the mercies of God, to come to God for help. Throughout the first eleven chapters of the book of Romans, Paul had established many facts and arguments to prove that God loves everyone, the entire human race. But despite all that God has done for us, those same chapters also reveal how proud men always go their own way, ignoring God and all He has to offer. With those two attitudes—God's love and man's sinfulness—proving to be dividing forces within the first eleven chapters, Paul brings us to chapter twelve where he proceeds to beg the people at Rome "by the mercies of God" to give God's principles for living a chance to work in their lives.

Hear the heart cry of Paul as you read Romans 12:1 and 2 once again:

> I beseech [beg] you, therefore, brethren, by the mercies of God [the truths I just shared with you in the first eleven chapters], that ye present your bod-

ies a living sacrifice, holy, acceptable unto God,
which is your reasonable service. And *be not conformed to this world*: but *be ye transformed by the
renewing of your mind*, that ye may prove what is
that good, and acceptable, and perfect will of God.

Paul fully understood how a culture's popular philosophies can distort our views and vision for living. Therefore,
Paul admonishes us in verse two to **"...*be not conformed to
this world*: but *be ye transformed by the renewing of your
mind*, that [we] may prove what is that good, and acceptable,
and perfect will of God."**

What exactly does that mean?

Simply put, we need to *renew* [reboot] *our minds* with
the Word of God so that our thought life lines up with reality—
*truth*—rather than the deceptive imagery we conjure up! Then,
God will give us the wisdom to see through the deceptive en-
ticements of our world to see the spiritual—God's purposes
and plans He has for us.

Since our society gloats in its sinful behavior, setting
forth imagery that attacks our computers (minds) every day,
sin is like a computer virus that creeps into the files of our
minds, shutting down essential functions that God original-
ly installed; that being, our imagination and our conscience.
Merely driving down the street looking at billboards or watching commercials on television can create major malfunctions
within our control center (conscience).

So, we have no other alternative but to purge and reboot.
According to Paul, it is a fundamental necessity. We need to
reboot our hard drives, trusting in God's Word to allow it, the

living water, to identify and cleanse away those deadly viruses from our files. And I want to add: this purge and rebooting process can only happen with a daily exercise called *prayer and meditation*.

There are many people reading this who have been Christians for years. They understand the necessity of using God's Word along with prayer to cleanse their mind.

Psalm 119:9 & 11 tells us: "Wherewithal shall a young man cleanse his way? by taking heed thereto according to thy [God's] word. Thy word have I hid in my heart, that I might not sin against thee…"

And according to Paul's procedure for cleansing, we need to take the first step as stated in Romans 12:1 which tells us to "present your bodies a living sacrifice, holy, acceptable unto God, which is our reasonable service."

Do you remember what Adam and Eve did immediately after sin entered their hard drives [heart and mind] when they heard God coming to visit them in the cool of the day? That's right. They *ran and hid themselves* from the only One who could remedy the situation *instead of running to God and presenting themselves to Him to ask for forgiveness.* In fact, they had the audacity to think they could hide their sin from a Sovereign God with a few fig leaves, knowing they were naked. They were convinced they could handle it. Look at Adam's life once again.

Prior to accepting sin as an alternative lifestyle, Adam was a man of great intelligence. In one day, he named every animal God had created. He was given great talents and abilities by his Creator. And yet, a second after he ate the forbidden fruit, he literally lost the capacity to think and reason properly.

Sin, which is *the source* of all guilt, fear, doubt, and shame, began running through Adam's brain like a destructive virus, turning him into a selfish and slanderous conspirator. Once sin was accepted, he did and said whatever he could to deflect the blame, convinced his cunning devices were justified in getting him out of this dreadful situation. It is obvious he didn't care who he hurt or who he slandered. He only cared about one person. And what's even more unsettling is how he tried to cast a negative reflection upon God's character in Genesis 3:12, "And the man said, The woman *whom thou gavest to be with me*, she gave me of the tree, and I did eat."

Let me paraphrase: "It was that woman *You* gave me… It's all *Your* fault, God!"

Oh, how different life may have been for all of us here on earth if Adam would have immediately run to God and confessed his sin instead of God having to go get him. And that's the way it has always been throughout the history of mankind. Although man is constantly running from God, His love for us puts Him in hot pursuit of every one of us.

Sad to say, we are no different than Adam. We're all sinners who have inherited the same destructive, prideful nature that keeps deceiving; even betraying, our conscience and imagination, our crucial mental files. And please, stop for a minute and consider; I mean honestly consider, all the wasted thought, sleep, and energy we burn up trying to deal with our sin. Whether our minds wander off into a fantasy world to escape or control our perspective of reality, or we become consumed by bad decisions we knowingly or mistakenly made, think what we could do if we would but harness and channel that wasted energy toward God. We need to just run to God!

Thank God, there is a solution to this crisis, and it is found in I Corinthians 2:9-16 where Paul tells us:

> But as it is written, Eye hath not seen, nor ear heard, neither hath entered into the heart of man, the things which God hath prepared for them that love him. *But God hath revealed them unto us by his Spirit*: for the Spirit searcheth all things, yea, the deep things of God. For what man knoweth the things of a man, save [except] the spirit of man which is in him? *even so the things of God knoweth no man, but the Spirit of God.* Now, we [as believers in Christ] have received, not the spirit of the world, but the spirit [a new software package] *which is of God; that we might know the things that are freely given to us of God.* Which things we also speak, not in the words which man's wisdom teacheth, but which the *Holy Ghost* teacheth; comparing spiritual things with spiritual. But the natural [ordinary, sinful] man receiveth not the things of the Spirit of God: *for they are foolishness unto him: neither can he know* [install] *them*, because they are spiritually discerned [in a fog]. But he that is spiritual judgeth all things, yet he himself is judged of no man. For who hath known the mind of the Lord, that he may instruct him? *But we have the mind of Christ.*

There it is: The new software package is *God's Spirit,* who gives us the mind of Christ when we're willing to receive it. However, did you also notice the danger that can prevent God from giving us His Spirit?

Paul told us the natural [ordinary] man "receiveth not the things of the Spirit of God: *for they are foolishness unto him: neither can he know* [install] *them,*" because they are spiritually discerned [in a fog].

What this passage is telling us is that some people have loaded their hard drives (hearts and minds) with so many worldly agendas, philosophies, and lusts within their imaginations that the things of God have become *"foolishness unto [them]; neither can [they] know them."* Their pride, excuses, and arrogance toward anyone who appears to be a threat blinds them from discerning what is true or false, and they especially reject anything that pertains to God, Who uncovers their error in judgment. It is heartbreaking to think that the majority throughout the world have no capacity whatsoever to even consider what the Lord has to offer them. They don't realize how they have become programmed and enslaved by their fear, skepticism, and resentment while making excuses for their guilt. Therefore, their quest to understand *who they are* within their possessions, achievements, and their vain imaginations has only distorted the truth, their reality. Their sin—as the Bible declares—has blinded them to who God is and what He has to offer them. This is the reason why it is vital for us to reconcile our imagination with the Sovereignty of God, with Who He is and what He wills for our lives.

To this point in our journey, I have presented you with many thought-provoking truths from the Bible, even some that may have challenged your views and beliefs. So, in a humble effort to bring clarity to what I have present to you throughout our journey, I want to give you two more scriptures I think you will be familiar with. And then, I want to share a story with you that will not only illustrate; but magnify for you, how dangerous it is for us to let our imagination wander outside the *boundaries of God's truth.*

First, in the gospel of John chapter 14, verse 6, we find the answer to the deep question Pilate asked Jesus the day he crucified the Lord: *What is truth?* Shortly before this event Jesus told Thomas, the doubter, "I am the way, *the truth*, and the life: no man cometh unto the Father, but by me."

And second, there is John 3:16 and 17 that reveal to us why Jesus came to Earth:

> For God so loved the world, that He gave His only begotten Son, that whosoever believeth in him should not perish, but have everlasting life. For God sent not His Son into the world to condemn the world; but that the world through Him might be saved.

# A Legacy for Larimore

INTRODUCTION

Without a doubt, the Lord Jesus Christ is the greatest teacher to ever walk upon the face of the earth. Many realize this as a fact, because He is God Himself. So, it only stands to reason that He would be the greatest teacher.

It is, however, interesting to note how His methods of teaching even stunned His enemies when they had to give a report to their superiors in John 7:46, "Never man spoke like this man." Other skeptics, after hearing Him teach, inquired of Him in Matthew 13:54, "[From] whence hath this man this wisdom, and these mighty works?" And yet, what interests me most is the question His disciples asked Him in Matthew 13:10, "Why speakest thou unto them in *parables*?" It seems He utilized parables when teaching rather than any other method. Why? Because parables grant us a better opportunity to grasp heavenly truths while meditating on His earthly illustrations.

Of course, the Lord used many other methods in His teaching ministry. He presented object lessons by multiplying a few fish and some bread to eliminate any doubt that He was, indeed, the bread of Life which came down from Heaven. He took many opportunities to heal people in order to reveal the misplaced priorities they had allowed to enter their lives. He also rebuked the winds and rain to show everyone who would trust Him that He can bring rest and peace during the storms of life. He even raised people from the dead so the world might know and have confidence that He is the Resurrection. I could go on and on.

The following parable [story] is a humble effort by this author to magnify for you, the reader, two profound truths:

First, it will reveal to us the deep-rooted resentment people have toward the Heavenly Father. Since many people fail to understand His specific plan for their lives, their hearts become sick when they experience any failure in their efforts to secure their coveted hopes and dreams. (See Proverbs 13:12.)

Secondly; and most of all, within this story we will see how the Heavenly Father, Sovereign God, literally emptied Himself into His Son to reveal to everyone His will. John 5:19 tells us, "The Son can do nothing of Himself, and He that honoreth not the Son honoreth not the Father." The heart of the Father is in the Son. May we truly come to realize the importance of honoring the Son since the Father has chosen Him to speak to us in these last days. (See Hebrews 1:1-2.)

# The Visit

Northwest of Richmond, Virginia, the small community of Larimore laid nestled in a peaceful, tree-lined valley. Though the residents of this quaint, little town were by the world's standard considered middle-class people, there was one man who dwelt there who was extremely wealthy. His name was Charles McManus. He had settled into this countryside community some years prior to its development; and yet, no one really knew anything about him. In fact, he was rarely ever seen.

But one thing was extremely clear. He protected his privacy. His mysterious and extravagant house, which sat way on top a hill overlooking the entire town, was surrounded by a huge, twelve foot, wrought-iron fence and gates that hedged his property. Then, of course, there were his four Dobermans that roamed the grounds, which truly kept everyone at a distance. Still, the entire township enjoyed the serenity of this newly-established community which only had a population of some twenty-four thousand people.

It was truly a prosperous and exciting place. Within a few short years, major factories had relocated there, giving the people great opportunities for employment. And since the residents had good-paying jobs available to them, the families flourished. Children filled the small town, and everyone was very happy and content. The town had several entertainment facilities, museums, and a concert hall where the orchestra played weekly, as well as an aquarium and zoo. Of course, the most exciting place for the children was the huge amusement park which attracted people from everywhere.

Larimore had quickly become an exciting little town to visit, and many tourists enjoyed the town's friendly charm. In fact, it was so appealing that many visitors entertained the thought of moving there. Unfortunately, the expanded town had already grown to its borders, making a move into Larimore virtually impossible. And to secure this end, the Mayor of this town, Michael Bowers, had convinced the entire township to implement new building codes, along with a voting process for accepting new residents. This would protect Larimore's future. And since the fifty-eight-year old Mayor had served this town so faithfully for the last twenty-eight years, everyone had total trust in him and his devotion to their township.

Of course, this beautiful, tiny haven of Larimore was not void of problems. The new building codes, along with the voting process for accepting new residents, created a sore spot for the town despite the protection it offered. Many long-time residents became resentful and aggressive when their efforts to gain the community's approval failed as they looked forward to seeing many relatives and friends move into their quaint, little town. And since the majority of the applicants were rejected, town meetings were very stressful at times. Ultimately, the people respected the township's detailed restrictions, realizing their town's preservation was more important than a few individuals.

During these disruptive moments, however, it was quite evident that Mayor Bowers was the bonding force which held this town together. His vision for Larimore, along with his sacrificial giving, promoted sincere harmony and unity among the people. Since Mayor Bowers was a bachelor and somewhat married to his town, he took upon himself the exhausting responsibility of visiting the residents on a regular basis in order to maintain unity and progress. He was always open to new ideas and listened patiently to problems, in order to minimize criticism and keep peace within his town. He especially made it his business to visit the few new families who settled into the city of Larimore.

One cool November evening, Mayor Bowers decided to pay a visit to the town's newest residents, the Kenzington family. They had only been in Larimore for a week, and their arrival was a surprise not only to the town's people, but also to the Mayor. No one knew of the Kenzingtons. Even the Mayor stood somewhat confused, knowing their acceptance as residents was never brought before committee or voted on by the community. But deep down in his heart he knew exactly how the Kenzingtons had gained entrance. For now, his concern for maintaining harmony within his town became a priority as he wondered how the township would react to their newest arrivals. Many residents began expressing their bewilderment, wondering how the Kenzingtons had gained entrance to their little haven without meeting the requirements of the current laws and regulations.

Arriving at the Kenzington home, the Mayor briskly walked along the narrow sidewalk and up the porch steps of the newly built Cape Cod. He soon found himself pausing, wondering how this family would receive him. It was difficult to keep his focus on this visit as the pressure of the residents' resentful attitudes dominated his thinking. Then suddenly, while admiring the floral wreath which hung upon the front door, he heard groaning noises coming from the other side of the front door.

"AAHHOO, MMAHH...we're going to have to get an electric chair, Honey. This is too, too difficult," echoed a man's voice within the foyer.

The Mayor didn't hesitate. He knocked despite the groaning. After a few moments and a second knock at the door, a huge, bearded man opened the door. He was a rugged-looking fellow and it was only the childish smile on his face that kept Mayor Bowers from becoming fearful of him.

"Hi. My name is Michael Bowers. I'm the Mayor of Larimore. How are you this evening, sir?"

"I'm just fine, thank you. My name is Gus Kenzington. Would you like to come in?"

"Certainly, I would like that," Mayor Bowers replied with surprise, as he was greeted so kindly. As the Mayor entered the home and followed Gus into the living room, he noticed a wheelchair and some walking equipment which set within a hallway leading to the kitchen. These items drew him to an obvious conclusion that someone living in the home had some sort of handicap.

Mayor Bowers looked to Mr. Kenzington and wondered, "I couldn't help but hear you groaning as I came upon your door. Is everything all right, Mr. Kenzington?"

"Yes, everything is fine." Mr. Kenzington assured him. "It's my daughter, Ruth. She recently lost the ability to use her legs, and it's been difficult adjusting to caring for her. I have to carry her around the house. You must have heard me taking her upstairs," he explained. "Come in and have a seat."

Just as the Mayor walked into the living room to take a seat on the couch, a beautifully-dressed woman entered the room from the dining room.

"Who was at the door, Gus?" she asked.

Just as she finished her question, she noticed the Mayor sitting on the sofa. "I'm so sorry. I didn't know you were here," she acknowledged.

Gus interrupted, "Rachel, this is Mayor Bowers. He's come to pay us a visit. Mayor, this is my wife, Rachel."

Mayor Bowers stood to shake her hand. "It's a pleasure to meet you, Mrs. Kenzington. I hope I'm not interrupting anything."

"No. Actually, you couldn't have come at a better time," she said graciously. "Could I get you something to drink, Mayor? Some tea, or juice?"

"No thank you, Mrs. Kenzington. And please, feel free to call me Michael."

"Thank you," Mr. Kenzington replied. "You may call me Gus, and I know Rachel prefers being called by her first name. Being called Mr. & Mrs. makes us feel old, anyway."

As Rachel smiled and nodded, the three of them made themselves comfortable in the living room. Michael, instantly taking a genuine interest, began asking Gus and Rachel a variety of questions for about a half hour or so regarding their move to Larimore and where Gus was employed.

Michael then asked. "Gus and Rachel, do you mind if I ask what happened to Ruth?"

"No, of course not," Gus responded. "Though it is painful to tell, I am so very proud of my little girl. We've just come from a small suburb outside of Georgia. It's been just over three months now...that's when it happened. Ruth was just walking down the street to a department store in town with Rachel; and then in an instant, a little three-year-old boy ran between two cars and out into a busy street. Because Ruth was admiring how cute the little guy was, she saw what was happening. So, she quickly ran across the street into the path of an oncoming car just in time to push the little boy out of its path."

Gus paused and began sobbing, placing his face in his hands. "She literally saved the boy's life, but the car hit her."

He continued while looking up toward the ceiling, "She may never walk again."

Though Gus freely told the story, Rachel sat in silence showing no emotion while staring at the coffee table. She was obviously in a state of shock as she recalled the incident.

"How old is Ruth?" Mayor Bowers asked.

Gus responded, "She'll be twelve years old next Friday."

"The doctors are sure she'll never walk again?" the Mayor questioned.

"They really don't know at this point. She is still recuperating from the initial blow. They said they'll know more in a few months."

"Well Gus and Rachel, I think you will find the people of Larimore very helpful and thoughtful of you. Please feel free to call on me whenever you feel I might be able to help in any way."

As the Mayor stood to leave, he had to ask one more

question. "One last thing, Gus. How exactly did you come about settling here in Larimore?"

"I kept receiving letters asking me to come," Gus answered. "To be honest with you, I don't have any idea where they came from or who sent them to me. The letters kept explaining to me that I could have this house mortgage free, and I could have a job working at the utility plant here in town," he explained in awe. "I'm just so thankful to whoever invited me here. Ruth's disability made it impossible for us to continue living in Atlanta with all the expenses from her accident."

Mayor Bowers stood up smiling, knowing exactly who had sent the letters to him.

"Gus and Rachel, on behalf of all the people here in Larimore, I want to welcome you. I know you'll adjust to our town and the quietness of it all. And again, if there's anything you need, please don't hesitate to give me a call."

As Mayor Bowers handed Gus his card and walked out onto the porch, Gus thanked the Mayor for his visit. Mayor Bowers, then, decided to pay someone else a little visit too.

# The Meeting

It was now late in the evening on this cold, dark night when Michael Bowers approached the McManus house that sat atop the hill at the edge of town. As he came upon what seemed to be a fortress, he merely opened the huge gate, stepped inside, closed and secured the lock, and then took the long journey up the sidewalk toward the grand house. The Dobermans loved these rare visits by Mayor Bowers since he brought them treats which he used to quiet them.

Once at the front door of this impressive stone mansion, the Mayor always chuckled as he could hear his knock upon the door echo through the hollowed foyer. The crescendo seemed to flow through the entire house.

Moments passed and then Mr. McManus, an elderly man in his late eighties, appeared at the door wearing a robe and slippers.

"What took you so long?" Mr. McManus questioned with a snicker.

"To be honest, I knew you had kindled another fire for me to extinguish, and I've been thinking about how I'm going to handle this one," Michael replied while the two of them strolled through the foyer and into the library.

As they stepped inside the library, the heat and smell

of the fireplace crackling provided an atmosphere of soothing comfort.

Mr. McManus slowly walked over to the side of the mantle. Reaching down to pick up a piece of wood to place on the fire, he prodded the Mayor while glancing back at him over his shoulder.

"You know, fires provide much warmth for those who choose to get close yet stay far back enough not to be burned."

Across the room, the Mayor flopped himself down on the sofa, draping his arms across the top of the camel-back leather frame and retorted, "Once again, your plans for this city are stirring up the township. Why didn't you at least tell me what you were planning before bringing the Kenzingtons into Larimore? You knew all the questions I'd be asked. I had a hard-enough time trying to explain to everyone why the house was being built."

"Everything will be fine," Mr. McManus assured him as he took a seat in a tufted, burgundy leather wing chair beside the fireplace.

He continued, "The Kenzingtons have settled in nicely, and Barlow has taken care of his job at the utility plant for me. Certainly, the people will ask questions they already know the answers to, but I'm very curious to see how they will receive the Kenzingtons. Have you met them yet?"

"Yes, I just came from there," Michael replied.

"Good!" Mr. McManus approved. "Then you know the hardship this man and his family have been through over the last few months. I read about them after hearing from a friend of mine in Atlanta. The Kenzingtons will be an excellent addition to this community. I just hope the people of this town will do their part to try to help them."

"Help them!" Michael exclaimed dauntedly. "I'm already hearing the rumblings and questions around town. Do you realize how this will disrupt this town?" Michael questioned as he leaned back on the couch.

"Nothing I've ever done disrupts this great town," Mr. McManus replied harshly. "Tell me one thing; not four or five...just one thing I've ever done that the people of this town haven't enjoyed and benefited?"

"I know. But what will I tell them at the town meeting next week?" Michael asked, seeking advice. "The Kenzingtons move into town will be the only thing we'll discuss...and you know it."

"You don't tell them anything this time," Mr. McManus said with a curious smile. "You don't answer one question. This time you'll ask all the questions."

"What are you talking about? Ask them the questions?" Michael replied, influenced by the attitude of the township. "Remember how peaceful it was around here eight years ago until you decided to build the zoo? Then, four years ago, you decided to create the mammoth amusement park. Have you forgotten what the people of this town put me through with that project?"

"I realize they have a resistance toward change," Mr. McManus replied as he leaned forward cupping his tea in his hands. "However, I've been noticing how many of the folks around this town are getting just a little too comfortable. Their attitudes have even become harsh toward the visitors. They seem to be losing heart."

"Yes," he stated with a twinkle in his eye as he leaned

back in his chair. "You'll ask all the questions next week. And be sure you listen carefully to their answers, my son."

"Dad, all I'm asking is that you tell me in advance why you are doing what you're doing so I can prepare the people in some way," Michael seemed to beg.

Slowly lifting himself to his feet, Mr. McManus walked toward the mantle with his eyes intently fixed upon the fireplace.

"Michael, I'm eighty-eight years old now, and I don't have much time to accomplish all I want to do. But I'll remind you of this one thing once again. After your mother and I adopted you, we decided to do everything within our power to make you a man who would have a sincere heart for others. From the moment we chose you from all the children at the agency, we wanted desperately to make you a passionate individual."

He continued as he turned, looking at his adopted son. "That's why I allowed you to keep your birth name, Bowers. Oh, how your mother insisted we change your name to McManus. Though there's nothing wrong with that, I just saw that as an act of pride rather than what was best for you. I never wanted you to forget that you were chosen by us. And I might add, keeping our relationship a secret thus far has certainly helped us serve this town better."

Taking a few steps toward his son, the elderly man began to recall the past. He seemed to fall into a trance.

"When your mother and I purchased this land where Larimore now stands, it was nothing more than useless wetlands. Yet, your mother and I shared the dream you are now living here in Larimore."

Walking back to the fireplace, he continued, still gazing intently while he spoke.

"After her death, when you were only nine years old, it became extremely difficult to keep our vision alive, as I needed help with you and your education. So, I sent you to the best schools and then on to college. I realized I had but a few short years to get this city off the ground. It was incredible to see how my financial backing and planning, along with the help of Barlow, Jones, and others within the City Council made your mother's dream and mine a reality."

He paused and then looked back at Michael.

"Before the meeting next week, I just want you to think about two things when you're walking around this great town. First, remember that forty-five years ago this town was nothing but a deserted meadow with hills and trees. Now, we've sprinkled in some happiness, excitement, and opportunity. And most importantly, I want you to really think about my past decisions and how difficult they were for you. Were those hurdles worth going over; even climbing over, as you now see how the people have adjusted to what was actually best for them? Change always brings discomfort, but everything I've done was for their best."

As Michael stood up before his father, he realized just how big the old man's heart was. He mused upon the great sacrifices he had made through the years. He had not only lost his wife, but he had literally lived the life of a hermit, as he felt he could best serve the people of Larimore from a distance. Intimacy was reserved for only a few...a very few.

"Dad," Michael said as he hugged the old man. "I sure wish I had your wisdom and understanding. But most of all,

I'm sure glad I'm your son and loved by you."

# The Conflict

The dreaded day had come for Mayor Bowers. Already frustrated and confused about the suspected outcome of the town meeting, he decided to walk rather than drive to the Town Hall where the town's citizens gathered to discuss their important business.

When he finally arrived at the beautiful building, he stood there in awe thinking about all his dad had accomplished for this great town. Looking up at the American flag which waved so gently before the deep, blue sky, the stars seemed to look upon it as if they were an anxious audience awaiting the final act. The building itself was made of polished, white stone and was extremely broad. Everyone knew this prodigious structure was a place where every decision made within its walls would stand—for every decision was indeed made by the people.

As Michael walked up the wide, pyramid-like steps to enter the building, he purposely delayed his arrival so he might casually enter the meeting room. This would give those who had arrived early freedom to speak. He hoped to get a flavor of what the others were thinking. Although there were many pressing matters to be discussed; past experiences taught him the Kenzington's arrival in Larimore would be the major topic for the evening...possibly the only topic.

As he walked through the front doorway of the building, Michael could hear the chaos coming from the conference room echoing through the long, narrow hall. The voices blended together to create a sound which resembled waves crashing upon a beach.

Michael came upon the conference room and stood just outside the door, hoping something he might hear would give him some direction. But the conversations melted together, preventing him from hearing a single voice clear enough to detect what was being said.

Taking one last deep breath, he pulled the door open and entered the chamber with a pasted-on smile, hoping to hide the anxiety he was feeling. Instantly, the commotion was silenced, and all eyes became fixed on him. Now, the only thing Michael heard was his heart beating in his chest as he began to sweat.

While pacing nervously toward the front of the room, he refused to make eye contact or acknowledge anyone. All he could do was stare at his empty seat behind the podium and briskly walk to his place, laboring to hold his pasted smile on the entire way. Though it took him only fifteen seconds to arrive at his designated spot, it seemed like an eternity. Once there, he placed his briefcase down on the long conference table to his left, where six board members were seated. To his right just beyond the podium, sat six other board members. Everyone in attendance seemed to peer at him with vicious expressions, reminding him of loaded cannons. Michael, being aware of the situation, realized all he needed to do was light the match, and all the anger, misunderstanding, and resentment would give way to a massive explosion.

Michael slowly settled into the arena of silence, pulling a file from his briefcase. Then, he stepped to the podium. As he looked up, the tension surrounding this moment literally plagued him with dizziness. He certainly expected some problems, but this was worse than he ever imagined.

Standing broad-shouldered as possible, he remembered his father telling him not to answer any questions. "You ask all the questions," he remembered him say. Yet, because he was so nervous, Michael made the mistake of altering his standard greeting to the people. He immediately blurted out a statement followed by a question that totally caught the people of Larimore unaware.

"I had an opportunity to meet with Gus Kenzington and his family this week. It's amazing what this man and his family have been through over the last few months. Did any of you get a chance to go meet them and introduce yourself to them?"

Since the question ripped through the assembly like a lightning bolt, he quickly added a qualifying statement.

"I only want to hear from those who have taken the time to meet them. Can anyone stand up and share with the rest of us where this family has come from and what all they have endured?"

The sobering question left everyone disarmed. However, within ten seconds or so of silence, a hostile voice responded from the rear of the room.

"I'd venture to say McManus has something to do with them being here!"

The audience began to stir when Michael quickly returned a reply. "So, what if McManus did bring them here? Have you taken the time to visit them to see what you can do to help them?"

The latter question wasn't even heard as the name Mc-Manus brought the bitterness and resentment the people had been suppressing over the years toward him and his wealth to the surface. The people were outraged.

Mr. Mathias, an ex-board member, stood and challenged Mayor Bowers. "The regulations outlined in our town's constitution forbid the Kenzingtons from settling in our town without following the proper channels. Are we now going to open our entire city to everyone who wants to settle here? Show me when we voted on their acceptance! What's going on here, Mayor?"

Michael wondered how to respond to Mr. Mathias, because he was correct in his statement. Yet, Michael's heart ached as he thought about how insensitive Mr. Mathias and the others were toward this family they hadn't even taken the time to meet.

Mr. Evans, another ex-board member also added: "Yes, Mayor! Many of us have had applications for our families and friends denied over the last eight to ten months. Much time and thought went into just getting them through the approval process. Now, Charles McManus decides he wants someone here and they just walk right in?"

There was much commotion as Mr. Evans continued. "I have to agree with the others and Mr. Mathias. We must stay within the regulations you set up, Mayor. Show us where we voted on the Kenzingtons being accepted!"

Although Michael had thought often about telling the people of his father's dream for Larimore, he never did. For some reason, he, Barlow, Jones, and the other City Council members, seemed to enjoy all the surprises for expansion even though the changes brought about this kind of controversy at times. And yet, dad seemed to have crossed the line this time. It appeared he was now going around the by-laws he established for this town. Plus, he wasn't just placing a building in his dream. He was placing before the people responsibility that they did not welcome nor want to consider.

Michael thought long and hard while the people continued their verbal, riot-like rebellion. Then, in his righteous indignation, he went on the offensive and decided to enlighten the people. He thought for a moment that he might appeal to their fears just long enough to quench the resentment that was brewing.

"Let me make one thing clear to you," Michael stated firmly, but respectfully. "For your information, Mr. McManus happens to own every bit of real estate here in Larimore. Sure, all of you are buying your homes with the mortgages you've borrowed and secured from Larimore Federal, but the property your homes are sitting on is owned exclusively by Mr. McManus. And I might add: He alone is responsible for the financial backing of Larimore Federal. He just happens to own the bank you owe the money to as well."

He paused, wondering if he was saying too much. Yet he was so tired of all the complaining and murmuring that found its roots in the bitterness and resentment they felt toward his father—a man who cared so much for them. His heart was terribly wounded as he thought once again about how the people of Larimore never even attempted to visit his dad or get to know him.

Michael continued, attempting to divert the negative attitudes with less offensive questions. He calmly asked them, "It appears to me no one here has ever thought about how this town was established. Who do think started this town? And who do you think put up all the money for the expansions that you have been enjoying over the recent years?"

The people were silenced and became extremely anxious.

"Let me ask you all one last question," he proclaimed boldly. "Have we, or have we not, benefited from all the past additions we've seen built within our town? Sure, many of you may have already suspected that it was Mr. McManus all along who had the Cultural Centers built as well as the Aquarium, the Zoo, and the Amusement Park. And why did he do it? So you and your families could grow closer together. He wanted to see to it that our fair city had the best. If I remember correctly, most of you harshly disagreed with all those projects. Yes, it took some time, but now you all realize the great benefits we've enjoyed because of those decisions. Now here we are again. Mr. McManus decides to reach out to someone who desperately needs our help, and what is your response? Selfishness!"

Most residents didn't want to hear Mayor Bower's logic. Many were furious and continued attacking the Mayor, reminding him they all needed to protect their city from growth. Most residents stormed out of the meeting, fretting over the very thought that Charles McManus owned the property where their homes had been built. And because of this, it now seemed he could do whatever he pleased. They now felt they had no control over their town or future.

Michael made a firm suggestion. "Let's at least agree to

meet back here the same time next week. And in the meantime, think about what has happened in the past, and how those decisions benefited our families and our community."

# The Tragedy

A few days had passed since the town meeting and Mayor Bowers was having trouble sleeping nights. Haunted by the grim outbursts and responses he received that evening, he wondered constantly what he could have said or done to bring about a better solution to the Kenzington issue.

Since he knew a long night lay before him; and it was only 7:30 p.m., he decided to visit the Kenzingtons to find out how the township may have been treating them over the last four days. Although Mr. Kenzington was working at the utility plant and arrived home about 8 o' clock, it would give Michael a few minutes to talk with Mrs. Kenzington. Hopefully, some of the people in town were reaching out to greet Gus and his family to show them some compassion and concern.

As Michael left his home to take the drive across town, he again thought about Ruth and her courage. He also began thinking about Mrs. Kenzington's courage to have left her home in Atlanta, along with the heartbreak she must be feeling in her new home without any friends. He tried to imagine what she must be going through. While imagining what Gus and his family were enduring, he wrestled with a host of emotions. Even though the drive across town was but ten to fifteen minutes, he became somewhat frustrated as his thoughts ran the gamut. One moment, he experienced deep, heartfelt compassion for the Kenzingtons. The next moment brought him negative and harsh disdain for men like Mathias who refused to accept any change they didn't initiate. His imagination was running wild, this all had become emotionally draining.

Then, as Michael continued driving toward the Kenzington's home, he could see thick, dark smoke ascending from the area where the Kenzingtons lived. At first, he thought it was only the smoke from a chimney, but then realized the belching of the smoke was more than just a chimney.

His concern flowed from his heart to his foot as he accelerated his car toward the cloud of smoke. To his astonishment, it was leading him directly to the Kenzington home, and he found himself driving right down their street and to their house. By this time, flames could be seen through the window of a second-floor bedroom.

Michael immediately pulled his car along the curb, and barely had it stopped before leaping out. He raced to the front door, but it was locked. He began to knock and yell as loud as he could. After a moment, Mrs. Kenzington answered the door with a laundry basket in her hands. It was clear she had been doing laundry in the basement and didn't realize her house was on fire.

"Mrs. Kenzington, call the fire department," Michael said firmly. "The second story of your house is on fire. Where is Ruth?"

Mrs. Kenzington couldn't believe what she was hearing. Dropping her laundry basket on the floor, she lunged toward the stairway to get Ruth.

Michael grabbed her and looked at her sternly. "Mrs.

Kenzington, get outside! I'll get Ruth." As he began running up the steps, he nervously asked, "What room is she in?"

Mrs. Kenzington began crying hysterically. "She's in the first room on the right just off the stairs."

Michael quickly ran up the steps but found himself running directly into a thick cloud of smoke halfway up. He couldn't see a thing. By the time he arrived at the top of the steps, he was totally blinded by the smoke and could now feel the heat coming from the flames.

"Ruth!" Michael yelled as he maneuvered his way toward her room.

By now, his endless coughing along with the fire engine sirens blaring outside made it difficult to hear if Ruth was even responding.

"Ruth, can you hear me? Ruth, please answer me!" he called once again.

There was no response.

Michael, having difficulty breathing while blindly searching for Ruth's room, was not only fearful for Ruth, but also felt a bit of panic as he began worrying about his own safety.

Becoming a bit frantic, he found the doorknob to Ruth's room. As he touched it, the heat from the knob indicated the fire was indeed in the room where she slept. When he opened the door, he found the room totally ablaze. The flames gave Michael just enough light to see Ruth lying on her bed as it was starting to catch fire. He continued coughing and gasping for air and began to get dizzy from the smoke. With all his might, he swept Ruth off the burning bed and cradled her in his arms as he ran for the door but tripped over a chair. He tried desperately to lift Ruth up again but failed, due to the pain he felt in his chest as he struggled for breath.

With one last, great effort, Michael lifted Ruth as he stood upon his knees. He was so weak from the struggle for air he just couldn't get back on his feet. The smoke surrounded him and Ruth now, and Michael collapsed.

Outside, the firemen arrived with their equipment. Mrs. Kenzington was standing safely on the sidewalk. She watched in terror as her home burned. She was crying as the neighbors huddled up the street, watching while the firemen quickly went to work. Not one person went to comfort Mrs. Kenzington.

"Mayor Bowers and my daughter are in the house," Mrs. Kenzington told one of the firemen.

"Do you know where they are in the house?" the fireman asked.

"They have to be upstairs," Mrs. Kenzington said, her hands trembling over her mouth. "Please hurry. They've been in there for almost five minutes."

The fire crew immediately began soaking the house with water. Four other firemen ran inside looking for Mayor Bowers and Ruth. It only took but a minute, and the firemen came out the front door carrying the Mayor and Ruth.

Mrs. Kenzington immediately ran to the ambulance where Ruth was taken. Many of the neighbors went over to see how Mayor Bowers was fairing as the paramedics cared for him at another ambulance. Although it was good to see them out of harm's way, Michael and Ruth didn't look well at all. They just lay on the stretchers motionless, their clothes covered in soot and burned in spots.

While Michael and Ruth were being placed in separate

ambulances, it was obvious the paramedics were trying to revive them. The smoke had done extensive damage, and the people could only pray they would be alright. The ambulances rushed off to Larimore General Hospital.

No one in Larimore slept that night as they thought about their great Mayor. Many phone calls were made throughout the night hours, as conversations reflected on all his hard work and devotion that made their city a place of happiness and security.

On the other hand, however, many people were venting their emotions in anger toward the Kenzingtons. They thought: "If they had not moved into Larimore, this never would have happened." It was very unfortunate. Most people felt anger rather than pity, due to the uncertainty they now faced regarding Larimore's future.

The next morning the local paper arrived announcing the terrible news on the front page:

## MAYOR BOWERS, OUR HERO, IS GONE!

The entire front page was devoted to telling the people of Larimore how their Mayor had saved young Ruth from death but lost his own life in the process. The investigation revealed the fire was caused by the medical equipment in Ruth's room. The wires were overloaded and sparked the flames in the drapes, which caused the blaze. The article went on to explain how Mayor Bowers had acted quickly enough to cover Ruth's nose and mouth with a thick sweater, allowing Ruth to filter her air just long enough for the firemen to rescue her. It appeared the sweater that saved Ruth's life was on the chair Mayor Bowers tripped over when exiting her room. Sadly though, the Mayor failed to find another piece of clothing to save himself. The article also explained in detail how Ruth had been injured during a heroic act in her hometown in Georgia just a few months prior to moving to Larimore.

Of course, the people of Larimore were devastated. In fact, every company, store, entertainment, and government facility closed their doors for the next few days until after the burial of their great friend. It was, indeed, hard to believe that this man could possibly be gone.

Unfortunately, Ruth and her parents once again had experienced great tragedy. Many of the folks in Larimore began showing sympathy toward the Kenzingtons, touching the hearts of Gus and his wife. After reading about Ruth's courage, many people took to heart the question Mayor Bowers had asked at the meeting just last week: "Did any of you take the opportunity to meet the Kenzingtons and introduce yourself to them?"

This tragedy would bring the people of Larimore together as the great compassion their Mayor had showered upon them penetrated their hearts and motivated them to action. Yet, there were more than a few in the fair city who were still outraged and hostile. They could only dwell on the thought: If it weren't for the Kenzingtons being here, we'd have our Mayor and everything would be peaceful.

The next few days found everyone emotionally numb as the funeral was organized. Of course, many wondered who would arrange the funeral since their Mayor had been a single man all his life.

# The Revelation

The day before the Mayor's funeral was a brisk November morning that brought a brilliant sunrise. As the people of Larimore awoke, they soon discovered their daily newspaper sitting on the end of their porches. Although the delivery of the paper was a daily occurrence, today's delivery demanded their attention. Usually, the newspaper ended up in the bushes, trees, or street. But on this day, they could not help but notice how the newspapers appeared to have been purposely situated on every porch regardless of whether the resident was a subscriber or not. Heightened curiosity led the residents to open the paper immediately. Some stood in awe as they read the headlines. Others ran to their telephones calling friends and family to see if they had read the headline of the paper which announced:

**The Entire Life of Michael Bowers**

**(A man after my own heart)**

**written by**

**Charles McManus**

This revelation caused everyone to put off any and all plans. Every family in the city gathered within their homes to read the twenty-seven-page newspaper that presented tremendous detail surrounding the life of their great Mayor, through the eyes of a man no one even knew. To their surprise, they would discover just how little they actually knew about Michael Bowers. Some would rejoice in hearing about all that had transpired in the life of their great Mayor. But others would reject the story, as they felt Charles McManus was trying to take advantage of the situation.

The story was a magnificent tribute to Michael Bowers. It revealed his entire life as a child, teenager, and young adult. Charles McManus withheld nothing from the people. He told them about Michael being adopted at the age of two. He explained why he never changed his name. He expressed how Michael had been the apple of his eye growing up, and how Michael graduated from college at the head of his class. He also revealed to the people how he had come to possess the land of Larimore, explaining how he and his wife dreamed of building the city they now had the privilege of living in for all these years.

While many people dissected the words within the paper, it was very disheartening that many felt no compassion for Charles McManus as he shared with them how he lost his wife to cancer when Michael was just nine years old. They only seemed to dwell on the fact that "they had been deceived" by many of the council members and board members who knew all about what was contained in the article. Harboring much resentment, many residents of the city found themselves bitter and angry. More than a few residents even spoke about forming their own committee to remove the existing board for defrauding the people.

The township soon found themselves very much divided over the story as they were preparing for Mayor Bowers' funeral to be held on Friday. When the discussion about Charles McManus' invitation within the paper arose, many chose to keep silent and merely try to evade the topic. But there were many despondent residents who went on a campaign, spreading scandalous rumors and accusations to persuade others not to attend the special Memorial Service Mr. McManus had planned to honor his son.

The invitation stated:

## ALL ARE WELCOME

I am extending to all the people of Larimore a special invitation to honor my only son, Michael Bowers. No one living outside of the city may attend this ceremony. It is exclusively for you, the residents of Larimore, who have had the privilege of being served by my son.

I cannot express the importance of everyone attending. The future of this great city will be announced. Anyone who fails to attend this special service for my only son will forever regret their decision not to attend. Your future will truly depend upon your being at this ceremony. The details for this special Memorial Service are listed as follows:

**Where: The Larimore Amusement Park
When: Saturday, the Sixteenth of November
Time: Gates will open promptly at Ten a.m.
Note: Gates will close at exactly Twelve Noon**

# The Memorial Service

On Saturday, the day after Michael Bowers' funeral, the entire town was in turmoil. Never in the history of this town had there been this much contention. Of course, everyone blamed Charles McManus. After reading his touching tribute to his only son in Thursday's newspaper, many people who started feeling for Charles McManus began doubting his sincerity, as he himself failed to attend his own son's funeral on Friday. No one understood why, nor was a reason given. For that reason alone, many who were reluctant to attend this day's Memorial Service at the park, made their final decision. They refused to answer the invitation of a man who would not attend the funeral of his only son.

Ten a.m. arrived and the gates opened at the Larimore Amusement Park. Many lines formed within the entrance stalls of the park, which extended through its large parking facility. Thousands had arrived early. Although many had come to pay their respects to Mayor Bowers, it was obvious some only came to satisfy their morbid curiosity.

Suddenly, an announcement was heard echoing through the park, giving detailed instructions to everyone regarding how they were to register prior to entering the park. Fear began gripping the hearts of the people as everyone was given a stern warning.

It was emphasized:

"Once you have signed in and entered the park, you cannot leave the park for any reason until the end of the service. If you make the decision to leave early, your name will be removed from the registration sheet. Then, your name will be placed on another list which will prevent you from re-entering."

Despite the fear and doubt some were experiencing as they suspiciously glanced at one another, they were compelled to enter and not turn back.

Once inside the park, the festive music soothed many of their fears and the residents began enjoying the activities that were made available. Mr. McManus had made provision so that every activity was free of charge. Every ride could be ridden. All the parlors, restaurants, and vending booths provided food at no charge. From the onset, all the celebrating was exciting, but again; it left the people feeling suspect. There seemed to be no room for mourning Michael's death.

However, just when the guests began reaching their peak of doubt toward Mr. McManus, they came upon the back side of the park where Mr. McManus had renamed one of the streets "Memory Lane."

The lane seemed endless as they looked down the long, straight pathway. Of course, it only took one glance and a few seconds to melt their anxious hearts. It was obvious what Charles McManus had done. Mr. McManus had enlarged sixty-six pictures he had taken over the years and placed them in chronological order along both sides of this one special lane. These huge portraits were strategically set to create a biography of Michael's life.

While they began viewing the first picture, they were instantly taken aback because it revealed Charles McManus with his beautiful wife, Margaret, standing in front of a huge, beautiful building. Not only was this their first introduction to Mrs. McManus, but a huge billboard within the picture set behind the McManuses displayed the name of a company—M & M Fuel and Oil, Incorporated. At the bottom of the portrait there was a caption giving a brief explanation. This first portrait disclosed to the guests how Charles McManus owned an oil company on the west coast and then sold the entire company. He and his wife, Margaret, felt deeply that running this company was pure vanity. They believed wholeheartedly in establishing a work that would affect the lives of others for generations to come.

The second picture showed the McManuses holding a youngster. Of course, everyone knew what this portrait was revealing before reading the caption. It was so obvious. It was a portrait of the day they brought Michael Bowers home from the adoption agency. The caption on this enlightening picture asked a question: "Will our son make a difference in the lives of others?"

While the guests continued strolling down Memory Lane, many other portraits revealed the dedication the Mc-Manuses had toward their new son whom they had chosen. One portrait everyone especially enjoyed showed Margaret and Michael when he was six years old at the base of a snow-covered hill. It showed how they had tumbled off their sled together at the end of a trip down the slope. They were both on their knees, covered in snow and laughing at one another.

The guests thoroughly enjoyed the pictures since they revealed a genuine and admirable relationship the McManuses had established in the early years with their son. But then, no sooner did the guests begin feeling secure in the truth they were discovering about the McManuses, their joy and security was shaken when they arrived half-way down Memory Lane. For at this point, there was a very sad and sobering portrait. Without warning, it invaded all the joyous moments and thoughts they had just experienced. It was a portrait of Margaret McManus with her obituary beside it. The explanation beneath the huge photo merely read: "My best friend was stricken with cancer and died just four months after she was diagnosed. Michael was just nine years old."

The hearts of the people began to melt. As they continued walking and thinking of what Charles McManus and Michael had gone through, the very next portrait showed Michael playing beside a pool with his mother. They were both holding hoses, squirting each other as they laughed and enjoyed their friendship as mother and son. The caption beneath this photo stated: "This picture was taken the day before Margaret was told by her doctors that she had just a few months to live."

As the people began weeping at seeing the sobering portraits, they came upon many other portraits that revealed a maturing Michael who obviously adored his father. He had achieved many awards growing up, and Charles McManus was by his side in every picture as Michael accepted his awards of achievement. Their relationship had deepened tremendously as they had both lost a great lady who loved them in a way they'd never know again.

Then, approximately three quarters of the way along Memory Lane, the people came upon huge portraits (aerial views) of what looked to be a virtual wasteland. It was incredible to imagine how this wasteland could give birth to the great community that rested in the heart of Charles McManus' imagination. Though the location was ideal for growth, the photos made you wonder how the McManuses could see a township within all the tree-tops and awkward hillsides. Yet, the caption read: "A Potential Promise Land...For all who will come."

After standing in awe of Charles McManus' vision and goals, the next photo displayed Michael graduating at the head of his class. By this time, you would expect nothing less from this man and his son as they became the closest of friends and partners in their quest to establish Larimore as a town to be admired.

The next series of portraits led the people through the early building stages of their town. You could clearly see how trees were removed, hills were literally leveled off, and streams were re-routed for beauty and pleasure. It was certainly not revealed in the captions, but the cost of all this developing crossed the minds of everyone who took the time to view the portraits. And finally, these portraits of Charles McManus' life had convinced everyone who attended this Memorial Service that this man was committed to this town and its people.

The next two portraits presented Michael taking the oath of office as Mayor. With his right hand in the air and a smile on his face, he had achieved the highest office in Larimore by fulfilling promises. While the people passed by these photos, they could not help but weep with joy as they realized

117

the greatness of this man who had truly loved them. Although his father helped him with the financial backing, it was his character and devotion alone that won the hearts of the people.

Memory Lane was a magnificent tribute to his only son, Michael Bowers. The people of Larimore cherished the portraits, which exhibited in tremendous detail Mr. McManus' focus and sacrifices to see his dream come true. They revealed how Michael's leadership stirred and secured the unity of the people to make this town so successful and prosperous. Everyone who chose to enter the park for this grand Memorial Service was blessed by Charles McManus' thoughtfulness.

However, time passed quickly as the guests within the park were viewing and pondering this fabulous tribute. It was now 11:55 a.m., and the outer gate to the park was about to be closed. Larry Jones, one of the city council members, stepped outside the entrance gate to make the final announcement:

"These gates will close in five minutes. Please come and sign in. Mr. McManus has so much more to offer you here in this town. I promise...you won't be disappointed."

The people who had refused to enter continued to yell harshly, "That man doesn't even have enough respect to attend his own son's funeral. He doesn't have a thing to offer us."

Others were hollering, "Everyone says he loves and cares for us. How can he care for us if he doesn't even love his own son? We're not falling for all that garbage he wrote in Thursday's paper."

Voices from within the rebellious crowd continued to resound, "It's all McManus' fault anyway. If he hadn't brought the Kenzingtons to our city, we'd still have our Mayor."

Others even jeered, "You're all fools to even believe

McManus and Michael were father and son. How gullible can you be?"

Despite the valiant effort by Mr. Jones to extend the last invitation, he could not be heard because of the emotional uproar that mounted.

He sternly warned them. "The gates will be closed in exactly one minute. You can enter the outer gates immediately and still have time to sign in for this special service. But I warn you; if you don't enter, you will regret it for the rest of your life."

Sad to say, no one came forward to accept the call. All who chose to enter had already come forward and had entered the gates.

The last minute had finally expired, and the people inside the park stood at the inner fence amazed. They watched the people who refused to enter begin pushing the gates closed exclaiming, "We don't want to come in!"

It was so sad to see such resentment and anger. Some of those just inside the gate began crying for those who displayed such hatred, even violent intent.

Inside the park, the activities continued for hours while people stepped up on the platform inside the pavilion to give testimony of how Mayor Bowers had helped them. Many of the people also gave witness to how the haven of Larimore encouraged them during their past moments of crisis. Most, however, expressed gratitude for the great opportunities and security the community provided. This was truly a great memorial service for their mayor and town that had prospered over the years solely because of their willingness to trust one man when tough decisions needed to be made.

The afternoon passed by so quickly. And then, a few minutes before 4:00 p.m., the entire park received an announcement from Mr. Barlow through the public address system.

"It's time. Everyone, please find your way to the pavilion immediately as Mr. McManus has arrived to speak with you. Please everyone...go at once."

It was a sobering arrival as everyone gathered into the huge pavilion that seated some six-thousand people. *Not a word was heard* as mixed emotions left the residents wondering what to expect. The shuffling of feet and movements from the affixed chairs resounded through the arena as the people were being seated. Many in attendance would have to settle for bleacher-like seating that was made available beyond the pavilion since the pavilion could not accommodate everyone. Fifteen to twenty minutes elapsed while everyone settled into their seats.

Then, without any fanfare or warning, Mr. Barlow and Mr. Jones, along with the other council members, walked onto the platform with an elderly man everyone perceived to be Charles McManus. The men on the platform all took their seats while Mr. Barlow walked to the podium.

Looking over the audience, Mr. Barlow smiled and opened the service.

"Over the last forty-five years, I've had the pleasure of working with Charles McManus. He has inspired, as well as directed, me and my family over these four and half decades. The vision he has brought to life in our fair city is an accomplishment never to be matched. And this vision was solely brought to reality through his devoted son who whole-heartedly gave himself to us and our town."

He continued. "Thank you all for coming today to celebrate the life of our beloved Mayor, Michael Bowers. We come to honor Michael and share our loss with a man who loved him so much more than we could ever have loved him. And now, you will get to meet the man who I believe is the greatest champion among men. Had Michael not fallen to this tragedy, I feared you might never have gotten to know the man I've come to know and love so much.

"I say all this because we are about to hear from Charles McManus publicly for the first, and maybe the last, time. So, without further delay, I present to you, my good friend and founder of Larimore, Mr. Charles McManus."

As Mr. Barlow walked across the stage to give Mr. McManus assistance, the cheers from the audience shook the entire park. Even the people outside the park who chose to reject the invitation could hear the excitement. And now, their curiosity forced them to gather around the outer fence so they might hear what was about to be said. For them—the thousands of people who stood outside the park—fear began to grip their souls; but outwardly, they tried to convince one another they had made the right decision, as they said one to another. "We'll still get to hear what's said. We didn't have to bow to this man."

Yet, despite all their attempts to encourage one another, the mockers outside the park were filled with fear and barrenness in the pit of stomachs and hearts. The cheers and unexplainable joy now being offered to a man no one had even met, left them wanting. And now, deep down in their hearts, many who rejected the invitation now wished they had entered.

On the platform inside the pavilion, Mr. Barlow arrived at the podium with Mr. McManus. The people could do nothing less than admire the elderly gentleman who walked with a cane. As Mr. McManus released his hold on Mr. Barlow's arm, steadying himself behind the podium, he looked out into the audience with a smile that literally brought tears to many as they cheered.

While Mr. Barlow politely adjusted the microphone to assist the shorter Charles McManus, Mr. McManus slowly raised both his hands in the air and the cheering crowd immediately became quiet. It was as though a thunderstorm had abruptly come to an end. The silence was indeed deafening.

After the silence had taken firm hold on the pavilion, Mr. McManus calmly placed his hands on the outside of the podium and began to speak with a soft, yet commanding voice.

"Yes, my heart is empty today because of the loss of my son, Michael. But your presence at this memorial service has brought me much joy as I have watched you today. Just to see the expressions of compassion on your faces as you took time to stop and look at the portraits has made this day so wonderful for me. You all have a great history to cherish."

He paused slightly, but then continued with a tone of sadness. "And you had to this point a great leader."

Mr. McManus began weeping and reached for a tissue that sat upon the podium. With a bit of tremor in his voice, he continued as he wiped his eyes.

"Michael would have been so proud to see you all come here today. He often asked me to have meetings like this. However, since many of my past decisions for Larimore had left many of you worried and even troubled, I felt it was best that

Michael handle them himself. And despite all the resistance he had to endure, his faithfulness to my plans has given you and your families tremendous privileges and opportunities."

Again, there was a brief pause as he wiped a tear from his cheek. Mr. McManus then continued speaking for some forty-five minutes, detailing the stories behind the portraits for the people and then finished with the reading from Thursday's newspaper article. Although he did not change anything in word, the people received the reading of the article as if they were hearing it for the first time.

At the conclusion of his rehearsing Larimore's entire history, his pause brought about a silence once again that seemed to invade the pavilion. The dominant hush that now gripped the entire pavilion was so arresting many could literally hear their hearts beating. Mr. McManus finally asked the obvious question.

"Where do we go from here?"

With his weakened voice, he continued. "Many would accuse me of taking advantage of opportunity. But I want to place before you today everything I know and have."

"First, when you arrived here in Larimore to purchase your homes, all of you secured your mortgages with Larimore Federal. I want you to know I personally own the banks and I alone am responsible for their finances. So for all intents and purposes, I still own your homes as not one of you has paid your mortgage in full to date."

At this point some became a bit nervous, wondering where this speech might be leading. And of course, the people outside the park who had been listening began casting terrible accusations against Charles McManus. What they were now hearing seemed to validate their negative opinions and hatred regarding this man and his "foolish vision" for Larimore.

"Finally," he continued as his weakened voice became more dynamic. "And this is the most important. I just happen to own all the land where your houses have been built. I own every inch of real estate in this town…even the property where the businesses and government offices reside."

Glancing over at the council members, he began laughing at the very thought of his vast wealth. "Isn't that something? And it amazes me that no one around here ever mentioned property taxes."

The entire assembly became troubled as it became obvious their future was sitting in the hands of this man. *Who in the world is this man? What are his plans?* they all thought as their skin tightened and their hearts began to pound with anticipation.

Mr. McManus smiled and continued. "As you know, in Thursday's newspaper, I invited everyone living in this town to this memorial service so that we might all honor my son, Michael."

Lifting his feeble hands over the audience, he asked boldly. "Is there anyone inside or outside this park who can honestly say they weren't invited? Let me know right now!" he demanded.

No one stirred as his boldness declared that no one had an excuse for not attending this service.

"That's right," he affirmed, while placing his hands back down on the podium. "No one can say they were not invited. Therefore, if you made the choice *not* to attend this memorial service, you chose not to honor my son and all he has done for you and this town. And those who have not come to honor my son have not honored me."

The people outside the gates became fearful and even began to panic as they heard those words. Some even began to look for a passage through the outer gate and fence so they might somehow sneak into the service. But it was impossible.

Mr. McManus continued. "I have thought long and hard over the last few days, and I have come to a decision that will stand and stand firm to its end. Unfortunately, there will be mixed emotions for many of you who are within this service. The good news is this: I have decided to give to you *who are here within this assembly and whose names appear on the registration sheets,* the land where your houses are sitting."

A thunderous gasp cut through the air but was silenced as Mr. McManus continued.

"I have already had the deeds set up for you and your families. All that is left to be done is to have your names placed on those deeds, and then my signature will gift my land to you. Of course, there is also the issue of your mortgages. I have also decided to forgive you of all your debt. Arrangements have been made to have your records reflect that payment has been made in full."

There was an incredible hush within the crowd as all were stunned to silence. They were shocked, thinking about the tremendous gifts being bestowed upon them. Many began weeping with joy thinking about this man and his generosity.

"Finally," he continued, "the sad reality of my decision? For the people outside this park who did not choose to honor my son, you will receive a notice from my attorneys. This notice will arrive no later than this Monday, the eighteenth, and it will demand payment for the property where your home resides. You are now required to pay one million dollars for the property where your homes are built, and it will need to be paid in full by Wednesday, November the twentieth at twelve noon. If payment is not received in full, you will then be served a notice demanding you to vacate your homes. At that time, any money you have paid toward your mortgages will be refunded to you entirely. Anyone who fails to comply with the notices will be punished to the greatest extent of the law."

The people outside the park heard this decision and became frantic as they desperately tried to get into the park. But there was no way to enter the huge gates and barbed wire fence. Others yelled at Mr. McManus through the fence.

"The property's not even worth one million dollars. You can't do this to us. How are we going to come up with one million dollars? There's no way we can pay that!"

A great sadness was felt inside the park. The horrible reality for the people inside the park was they had family and friends who chose to reject the invitation and stay outside the park. Despite all their efforts over the last few days to persuade them to come to the service, the pride, anger, and resentment that filled their hearts toward Charles McManus just could not be penetrated. And now, they would literally be banished from living in this great town that had done so much for them.

As Wednesday the twentieth arrived, no one could pay the debt they owed. Many people who were required to pay for their property had tried over the last few days to visit Charles McManus. They made every effort to visit him at his home so they might beg for forgiveness, as they had so wickedly accused him of having ulterior motives. Many letters were also written, hoping they would be considered. Yet, all and any pleas to Charles McManus were discarded. Therefore, all the people who did not have their names written on the registration list from the memorial service were banished from the great city of Larimore and not permitted to return.

Needless to say, those who chose to honor the son of Charles McManus went on to enjoy the city of Larimore and all it had to offer. Many new people were invited to move into the city, and Charles McManus continued to build up the city not only in concrete and mortar; but more importantly, in spirit and in truth.

Just three years after the death of his son, Charles McManus decided to move back to the west coast to spend his remaining days with family he had not seen for some years. It was indeed a sad time for all the residents of Larimore, for they had come to know and truly love this man's heartbeat.

Just a few weeks before his departure, Mr. McManus stood before the people at the pavilion for the last time, setting before the people a book which he had written over the years. It possessed not only the historical events of Larimore, but it also outlined in detail all the principles, restrictions, and guidelines he had used to govern his quaint and peaceful town. Thousands of copies of the book were published and distributed to the people of Larimore. He insisted they study it so they might insure the future of their great town.

After his departure, the passing years proved to the people of Larimore just how wise Charles McManus was. When the people obeyed the laws, guidelines, and regulations of the book he had written, the town prospered and the people were united. On the other hand, however, when the people or the

City Council violated the laws, guidelines, and regulations within the book, problems would surface, bringing about much contention and disunity.

Though much time has now passed since Charles McManus' departure, the people of Larimore often remember him and his son when making decisions for their town and in their personal lives. And even though the book became the center of much controversy at times, when difficult decisions arose, it not only proved itself worthy to serve the people, it also gave tremendous insight to the residents, reminding them of the love that motivated the founder of their town.

So, for now and forever, the people of this quaint, little town will always appreciate and cleave to this great book and the memories they possess in word and deed—*A Legacy for Larimore*.

# Conclusion

It was quite obvious that Charles McManus dealt harshly with the people who failed to accept the invitation extended to them for his son's memorial service. Though it may appear to be extreme, the people failed to realize that Charles McManus had given his *entire life* to them through the promotion of his son. Therefore, when they failed to honor his son, they also failed to honor the man who had given them everything they possessed. If it weren't for Charles McManus and the opportunities he set before them, they would not have had the privileges they experienced in Larimore.

The Lord God who created the heavens and the earth has also set before the entire world portraits of His love for us. All anyone needs to do is step outside one clear evening or day, and "the heavens [will indeed] *declare* the glory of God, and the firmament *showeth* His handiwork. Day after day *uttereth speech*, and night unto night *showeth* knowledge. There is no speech nor language where *their voice* is not heard" (Psalm 19:1-3).

Have we taken the time to stop and admire the portraits our God has set in His creation for us? His love, power, mercy, and faithfulness will clearly be seen if we would just take the time to go down God's Memory Lane.

God has also given to us *His Son,* who chose to come down from Heaven and give Himself for us. For some three and a half years, He went throughout the world inviting everyone to accept His invitation to eternal life. Of course, we know what man's response was to His invitation.

John 1:11-12 tells us: "He came unto His own, and *His own received Him not. But* as many as received Him; to them gave He power to become the sons of God, even to them that believe on His name."

Last, but not least: Although the Lord Jesus Christ is not here on earth in a bodily form, He and His Father have left us with a tremendous legacy. We not only have His portraits set before us in His creation and in the life of His Son, we also have detailed explanations [captions] written in a wonderful Book that outlines for us their laws, guidelines, and principles for living. Our success and happiness here on earth depends on our willingness to obey the legacy that has been set before us.

# Invitation

The Lord is preparing a home for ALL who will trust Him. There is so much He wants to do for us here, and after death. Unfortunately, people—like the doubters in Larimore—refuse to believe so they might enter into His Rest and all God has given them (The Bible) so they might have the eternal life that He has secured for them. Please note these verses:

Revelation 3:20: "*Behold, I stand at the door, and knock*: if any man hear my voice, and open the door [of his heart], I will come in to him, and will dine with him, and he with me."

Isaiah 55:6: "Seek the Lord while he may be found, *call ye upon him* while he is near."

Isaiah 1:18: "*Come now*, and let us reason together, saith the Lord: though your sins be as scarlet, they shall be as white as snow; though they be red like crimson, they shall be white as wool."

Matthew 11:28: "*Come unto me* [Jesus] all ye that labor and are heavy laden, and I will give you rest."

Hebrews 1:1-2: "God, who at different times in history and in different manners spoke in times past unto the fathers *by the prophets*, Hath in these last days *spoken unto us by His Son*."

John 3:36: "He that believeth on the Son hath everlasting life: and he that believeth NOT the Son shall NOT see life, but the wrath of God abides on him."

I realize there are many who reject this great Legacy we have before us. And it is sad to think that just as the people of Larimore were banished because of their unbelief, so will the people who reject the Lord Jesus Christ be banished from all that God has prepared for them.

Finally, we read in Matthew 10:32-33: "Whosoever, therefore, will confess me [Jesus] before men, him will I confess also before my Father, who is in Heaven. But whosoever shall *deny* me before men, *him will I also deny* before my Father, who is in Heaven."

His invitation is always open. Will you come and trust the Lord Jesus Christ who has given you His all...everything for you?

If so, all you need to do is ask Him. God tells us in Romans 10:9: "That if you will confess with thy mouth the Lord Jesus, and will believe in your heart that God hath raised Him from the dead, *you will be saved.*"

God also promises us in Romans 10:13, "Whosoever shall call upon the name of the Lord [Jesus] shall be saved."

Right now, I hope you will offer up a prayer to the Lord from your heart, asking Him to forgive you of your sins and to come into your heart to be your Savior so you will go to heaven when you die. But if you have trouble doing that, let me help you. And once you have prayed the prayer, feel free to keep talking the Lord. That's what it is all about!—Walking with your Creator as He has been dreaming about walking with you even before He created the foundations of the world.

Just bow your head and utter this prayer to Him.

Lord Jesus, after reading all of what has been shared, I had no idea how far away I have drifted from the reality of You. And, although I do understand a bit more about Your love for me, I never realized how by making a choice to deny and reject You, I have made a choice that will banish me from heaven. I want to say that I am sorry I always tend to blame You and others for my problems. So, I want to confess to You that I am a sinner worthy of death and hell, realizing now that I desperately need You to forgive me of my offenses. I understand now that You, Lord, have given me everything I have, and I've been extremely selfish, giving You nothing. Please forgive me of my sin and come into my heart today and help me to follow You. As best I know how, I ask You to do this. Please help me to believe and trust You more as I try to study Your Bible and live for You. Thank You for Your goodness and mercy, and please help me to see more clearly what I am to do until I meet You on the other side. Amen.

If you have prayed and ask the Lord to forgive you so He might guide you through this life and into His Heaven when you do die, look at the confidence you can have in Him:

> Hereby *know we that we dwell in Him, and He in us*, because He hath given us of his Spirit. And we have seen and do testify that the Father sent the Son *to be* the Saviour of the world. *Whosoever shall confess that Jesus is the Son of God, God dwelleth* in him, and he in God.

1 John 4:13-15

And this is the record, that God hath given to us eternal life, and this life is in his Son. *He that hath the Son hath life*; *and* he that hath not the Son of God hath not life. These things have I written unto you that believe on the name of the Son of God; *that ye may know that ye have eternal life*, and that ye may believe on the name of the Son of God.

1 John 5:11-13

Second Peter 1:3 and 4 tell us about God's gift of His Spirit:

According as *his divine power* [His Spirit] hath given unto us all things that pertain unto life and godliness, through the knowledge of Him [Jesus Christ] that hath called us to glory and virtue: *Whereby are given unto us exceeding great and precious promises:* that by *these [promises] ye might be partakers of the divine nature*, having *escaped the corruption* that is in the world through lusts.

But if you are still on the fence, not sure about making the choice to believe and accept Jesus Christ as your Savior, I want to remind you of the battle going on in your soul and spirit. Here are some verses I hope you will humbly read:

Solomon tells us in Proverbs 28:13, "He that covereth [makes excuses for] his sins shall not prosper: but whoso *confesseth* and *forsaketh* them shall have mercy."

Romans 3:23 makes it even clearer... "For *all have sinned* [rebelled against God] and come short of the glory of God.

Romans 6:23 tells us, "The wages [payment given] of sin is death, but the gift of God is eternal life through Jesus Christ our Lord."

Look at Revelation 21:8:

> But the fearful, and *unbelieving,* and the abominable, and murderers, and whoremongers, and sorcerers, and idolaters, and *all liars*, shall have their part in the lake which burneth with fire and brimstone: which is the second death. [Separated from God.]

Romans 5:8 says this, "But God commendeth [proved] His love toward us in that *while we were yet sinners, Christ died for us.*"

Second Corinthians 5:21 declares, "For He [God] hath made him [Jesus Christ] *to be sin for us,* who knew no sin; that we might be made the righteousness of God in him."

Matthew 20:28 says, "Even as the Son of man came not to be ministered unto, but to minister, *and to give His life for a ransom many.*"

It was His Holy Life—alone—given on the Cross, that became the payment for our sin, to ransom us from sin's penalty.

First John 1:9 assures us of God's forgiving Spirit for, "If we confess our sins, He is faithful and just to forgive us of our sins, and to cleanse us from all unrighteousness."

John 1:12 tells us, "That He [Jesus] came unto His own [the Jewish Nation], but His own received Him not; *but as many as received Him, to them gave He the power* [His Spirit] *to become the sons of God.*"

[God] hath delivered us from the power of darkness, and hath translated *us* into the [*eternal*] kingdom of his dear Son: In whom we have redemption through his blood, *even* the forgiveness of sins: Who is the image of the invisible God, the firstborn of every creature: *For by him [Jesus] were all things created,* that are in heaven, and that are in earth, visible and invisible, whether *they be* thrones, or dominions, or principalities, or powers: *all things were created by him, and for him: And he is before all things, and by him all things consist.*

Colossians 1:13-17

First Peter 2:24 says, "He himself bore our sins in His body on the tree, that we might die to sin and live to righteousness. By His wounds you have been healed."

Here's the passage of scripture that dropped me to my knees. After falling into the temptations of the 60s and 70s culture that exhorted us to fulfill the lusts of the flesh, it's not hard to figure out where I was living in the list below:

*This* I say then, Walk in the Spirit, and ye shall not fulfil the lust of the flesh. For the flesh lusteth [wars] against the Spirit, and the Spirit against the flesh: and these are contrary the one to the other: so that ye cannot do the things that ye would.

But if ye be led of the Spirit [of God], ye are not under the law. Now the works of the flesh are manifest, which are *these;* Adultery, fornication, uncleanness, lasciviousness, Idolatry, witchcraft, hatred, variance, emulations, wrath, strife, seditions, heresies, Envyings, murders, drunkenness, revellings, and such like: of the which I tell you before, as I have also told *you* in time past, that they which do such things shall not inherit the kingdom of God. *But the fruit of the Spirit is love, joy, peace,* longsuffering, gentleness, goodness, faith, meekness, temperance: against such there is no law.

Galatians 5:16-23

Although we humans can be complicated beings, there are but *three things* we all crave and long to embrace above all else, and they are listed here and given to us by only one Source—God's Spirit! And these are: Love, Joy, and Peace.

If you're like me, that's all I want! Certainly, these three will be rattled and tested by life's trials, temptation, suffering, and pain at times. But if we RUN to the Lord during those times, He promises He will see us through them all.

## Finally

It's time to stop running from the Lord and run to Him as often as you can. Start by getting a Bible and reading the Gospel of John (the fourth book in the New Testament) at least two times all the way through, asking Him to open your eyes to the truth about Jesus Christ, along with the sinfulness of man. After you have read this Gospel twice, go to the beginning and read Genesis and Exodus, where you will discover God's heart within the affairs of men. Feel free to help yourself to the Book of Psalms and Proverbs along the way. The Lord will give you tremendous insights for your meditation that will help guide you around the deceptive mental roadblocks you have built within your heart and mind via your imagination over your lifetime.

And you might put these verses to memory:

Proverbs 3:5 and 6: "Trust in the Lord with all thine heart; and lean NOT unto thine own understanding. In all thy ways acknowledge Him, and He shall direct thy path."

I'll close now and ask you one final question.

I hope you have admitted that you have within your heart and mind a destructive virus called "sin" that magnifies your fears, doubts, and pride. If you have, don't ever be like Adam and Eve again, who ran from God when they disobeyed Him. Oh, how different Adam and Eve's future would have been IF they would have just run to God when they messed up rather than away from Him to cover it up.

As we come to the finish line, the reality is, my friend, you are going to mess up again as we all do, because old patterns are hard to break. But remember: If you have accepted the Lord Jesus Christ as your Savior, you are now God's child and He promises us that He will never leave you or forsake you.

The Lord God who knew ALL about you before you were even born already knows what you've decided. He even knew what you were going to decide before He laid the foundations of the Universe. But remember: Once you die on your appointed day; and that will be one appointment you will NOT be late for, eternity will echo forever and ever and ever from your lips one of these two statements I shared with you in my poem, "I'm sure glad I did." or "I sure wish I had."

So, have you accepted the Lord Jesus?

# About the Author

Thank the Lord my wife, Carol, and I came to accept the reality of Jesus Christ! Although there is much I could share with you, it is enough to say that we did not come to accept the Lord's cleansing power until after our teenage years had made havoc of our lives. Our hearts and minds were greatly damaged by the sexual and prosperity revolutions of the 70s and 80s.

Prior to accepting the Lord as our Savior, we were both blinded by the world's empty promises. I had adopted the philosophy of the sixties and seventies, believing that the sex, drugs, and rock-n-roll lifestyle was my ticket to paradise and freedom. Carol, on the other end of the spectrum, became extremely ambitious in her career, while enjoying her purchasing power. How did this happen within our lives?

While progressing through my teenage years, I experienced many failed attempts to establish the ultimate relationship with a woman. So, in order to comfort and relieve the hurt, emptiness, and other viruses that ate at my soul, I chose to hide behind my lifestyle while trying to shield myself from the bitter realities of life. Even though I enjoyed five different groups of friends, attending concerts on a monthly basis, and nightclubs four times a week while participating in seasonal sporting events, playing in hockey and softball leagues, along with water-skiing and vacations to the beach, I could never find the peace and joy my heart longed for. And the sad reality is this: I didn't even know what my heart was thirsting and hungering for until I came to accept what the Lord had done for me at the Cross. When I asked the Lord to forgive me of my sin on a Wednesday night, October 22, 1980, the love, peace, and joy I had been craving flooded my soul and I've never looked back.

Carol, on the other hand, had also been hurt. She was forced to cancel two marital engagements due to her fiancés' lack of commitment. Since she was left believing you can't trust anyone but yourself, she channeled all her efforts into her career hoping it would give her life purpose and meaning.

But then, there was a day when she also came face to face with the Savior who told her in John 3:3: "Verily, verily, I say unto thee, Except a man be born again, he cannot see [comprehend] the Kingdom of God."

Carol was twenty-one years old, and I was a month shy of my twenty-first birthday when we discovered the way of the Cross leads home. And thank God we did! Both of us had certainly seen enough of the world to realize there is no hope or love found there. The world is a burdensome taskmaster that only cares about itself. But when we both found ourselves in a Bible-believing church where Christ and His kingdom were exalted, we didn't hesitate to run to the hope of having our lives cleansed and changed anew.

CPSIA information can be obtained
at www.ICGtesting.com
Printed in the USA
BVHW050642171019
561331BV00004B/18/P

9 781640 884434